Praise for *Sex Trafficking Prevention*

"As part of my role as a Vice President for the International Association of Trauma Professionals and CEO of the Arizona Trauma Institute, I have had the pleasure of interacting with Savannah. Her passion for ending sex trafficking and the exploitation of children have earned my respect and admiration. Savannah Sanders has been and will continue to be a powerful voice for policy and social change. I am pleased to be in a position to recommend her new book to you, and know that you will find that it is written in an easy and accessible format making the concepts and call to action clear and possible."

—**ROBERT RHOTON**, Psy.D.; LPC; D.A.A.E.T.S.
Diplomate of the American Academy of Experts in Traumatic Stress; Vice President, International Association of Trauma Professionals; Co-editor of *the International Journal of Trauma Practice and Research*; CEO of Arizona Trauma Institute & Therapy

"As a survivor and social worker, Savannah Sanders is a leading expert on the topic of commercial sexual exploitation of children (CSEC). Her book, Sex Trafficking Prevention, will be a great contribution to the anti-trafficking field. We are lucky to have such access to her insight and expertise. I am so proud to know her both professionally and personally."

—**HOLLY AUSTIN SMITH**, author of *Walking Prey*

D0198121

"Would you know how to recognize a child that is vulnerable to sex trafficking? Would you know what to do if you did? Sex trafficking of children is not the purview of third world nations nor is it something that happened in the past before technology was available to track predators. It's happening today ... in your city ... in your community ... every single day. That is one of the key messages imparted in *Sex Trafficking Prevention*, a powerful new book by survivor and prevention advocate, Savannah Sanders. By sharing her story Savannah opens our eyes to the world of childhood abuse and trauma that diminishes a child's feelings of self-worth, so much so that saying no and escaping the victimization become impossibilities. But this is not inevitable. We can do something to help at risk children. That is Savannah's other message. And through her book, she teaches us how. "

—**STEFANIE ZUCKER**, child health and safety advocate, Managing Director of Pediatric Safety, pediatricsafety(dot)net

"Given how horrible sex trafficking is, we don't want to think that it could ever happen to those we love. Yet as Sanders shows, any person is at risk, especially those who have been sexually abused as children. This books gives you the framework and tools to help develop your child's resiliency to sexual abuse in case they are targeted and builds their trust in you as a safe person to turn to. I hope this life-saving information will soon be implemented in every household, for every child.

— **SANDRA KIM**, Founder of Everyday Feminism

"This book is written with the same honesty and strength with which Savannah lives her life. Her ground-breaking book serves to remind us all that sex trafficking is a multi-faceted issue. Savannah bravely shares her experiences to educate readers about the link between sex trafficking, child abuse and domestic violence. Every advocate for child abuse and domestic violence must read this book. And every person who cares about others should read this book, and become a part of the solution through learning and being able to recognize the signs. Savannah's insight and advice throughout this book will no doubt save lives if readers are brave enough to utilize her wisdom and speak out. As a fellow advocate for victims, I feel confident we are making change with a woman like Savannah on our side!

—JESSICA NICELY, author, *Baba's Daughter*, CEO/Founder, Winged Hope Family Advocacy Foundation

"When we violate the sacred boundaries of childhood by sexualizing, raping or abusing our children we set them on a course vulnerable to the prey of unscrupulous pimps and johns. The FBI estimates that over 100,000 children and young women are trafficked in America today. They range in age from nine to 19, with the average being age 11. This glimpse into Savannah Sander's heroic story can help raise awareness, break down barriers to reality, and inform parents, police, educators and the legal system how to protect our children from sex trafficking."

—LYNNE KENNEY, PsyD Pediatric Psychologist, co-author, *BLOOM: 50 Things to Say, Think and Do with Anxious, Angry, Over-the-Top Kids*

SEX
TRAFFICKING
PREVENTION

A TRAUMA-INFORMED APPROACH
FOR PARENTS AND PROFESSIONALS

SAVANNAH J. SANDERS

3 1336 10084 0132

UNHOOKED BOOKS
an imprint of High Conflict Institute Press
Scottsdale, Arizona

Publisher's Note

This publication is designed to provide accurate and authoritative information about the subject matters covered. It is sold with the understanding that neither the author nor publisher are rendering legal, mental health, medical or other professional services, either directly or indirectly. If expert assistance, legal services or counseling is needed, the services of a competent professional should be sought. Neither the author nor the publisher shall be liable or responsible for any loss or damage allegedly arising as a consequence of your use or application of any information or suggestions in this book.

Copyright © 2015 by Savannah J. Sanders
Unhooked Books, LLC
7701 E. Indian School Rd., Ste. F
Scottsdale, AZ 85251
www.unhookedbooks.com

ISBN: 978-1-936268-84-9
eISBN: 978-1-936268-85-6

All Rights Reserved.
No part of this book may be reproduced, scanned, or distributed in any printed or electronic form without the express written permission of the publisher. Failure to comply with these terms may expose you to legal action and damages for copyright infringement.

Names and identifying information of private individuals have been changed to preserve anonymity.

Library of Congress Control Number: 2015944781

Cover design by Gordan Blazevik
Interior design by Jeffrey Fuller, Shelfish.weebly.com

Printed in the United States of America

DEDICATION

For Adrienne,
I hope this book helps
those you did not get the chance to help.

For those who have lost their way
because of trauma, and for
my children who exemplify
the change we want to see in the world.

Contents

Introduction 1

My Story 7

Chapter 1: What Exactly is Child Sex Trafficking? 27

Chapter 2: How and Why Trafficking Happens 43

Chapter 3: Groomed on Mulberry Street............................. 63

Chapter 4: How We Can All Intervene 81

Chapter 5: Signs and Prevention Efforts for Teens 93

Chapter 6: Healing and Overcoming Trauma....................... 109

Conclusion 127

Resources and Recommendations.................................... 141

Endnotes 144

Acknowledgements 146

About the Author 148

INTRODUCTION

The first time I came across the term "sex slavery," I was twenty-five years old. Scrolling through my Facebook feed, my eyes caught the headline of an article claiming to tell the harsh truths of human trafficking. As I read, I was struck with the shocking definition of sex slavery: The act of forcing or manipulating another person to have sex for the monetary gain of someone else. While this differs slightly from how the federal government officially defines sex trafficking, that simple definition turned my world upside down and started me on an incredible, emotional, and sometimes very frustrating journey of discovering one of the hardest truths of my life.

I had been a sex slave.

Sitting in front of my computer that day, I finally had something to call it—a name for the belittling and traumatizing experiences that caused me so much pain and inner turmoil even then, when it was all over. In one mindless moment of scrolling through social media, my life changed and I saw myself as a victim of sex trafficking. While I didn't understand exactly what had happened to me, the terrorizing memories prompted me to do anything I could to prevent another person from those experiences.

Still stunned, I called the organization referenced in the article and offered to volunteer. As the man who answered asked me basic questions about my interest in the organization, I started to cry as all the experiences I had kept locked in the back corners of my mind came tumbling out to land in the ears of a stranger. The man didn't say much; he just listened and allowed me to ramble. It was the first time I had ever told anyone about what had happened to me.

Toward the end of the conversation, I did something that I later learned was common among victims of trafficking and assault: I questioned if I was really the victim, or if I was the one to blame. Was it because I was not wearing the right clothes or because I was somewhere I shouldn't have been? I rationalized out loud, saying, "I don't know, maybe I wasn't a victim . . . I didn't run and I didn't fight. I should have fought or said no or done something." I continued down this train of thought, processing the conflicting feelings I was having. I told him, "Well, I was only sixteen and he was a grown man. But I thought I was grown at that time . . . ."

Now the man from the anti-trafficking organization interrupted me. "Hon, I don't know you or your story, but I do know that there was no way that any of that was your fault." That comment had a profound effect on me, and has stayed with me as I wrote this book. I believe it will stay with me for the rest of my life.

Child sex trafficking is one of the hottest social issues at this time in history. More and more media outlets are running stories on the problem, informational classes are being taught to various professionals, books are being written by survivors and experts, and everyday people are sharing what they have learned with others in their lives. Yet, as popular as this topic has become and as much momentum as we have gained in our anti-trafficking efforts, we still have a long ways to go in educating the public about the realities of trafficking and in communicating that we all have a role to play in preventing it.

Even the definition of "sex trafficking" is still unclear—

it is often confused with human smuggling and pictured as something that either happened a long time ago or something that does not happen now in Western culture. It is no surprise that many people have no idea that trafficking occurs in their own communities. Almost every time I tell someone about the advocacy and prevention work I do in the United States, I am faced with the same basic responses: One, I thought that only happened in Thailand, and two, why don't they run away from their kidnappers? We Americans, as a country but also as human beings, need to come to a point of truly understanding first what trafficking is and second—most importantly—that there is prevalent and urgent action everyone can do to stop it now.

We need to shift the global focus from talking about how terrible it is that trafficking exists to accepting its existence and begin prevention initiatives and programs that help victims find healing. As with any movement in its infancy, lots of mistakes are being made on the road toward developing real solutions.

Brief Overview of Trafficking

Listen to the evening news report or open a news app on your smartphone and you're likely to hear or see various terms about child sex trafficking. These may include domestic minor sex trafficking, sex tourism, survival sex, commercial sexual exploitation of children, and, modern-day slavery. All of these terms refer to the abuse and exploitation of minors (those under age eighteen), who are victims of sex crimes.

For the sake of simplicity, I will use the terms *sex trafficking* and *child sex trafficking* throughout this book. (A term I will not use is *child prostitution*, which implies that the child is a criminal instead of a victim.) The Trafficking Victim Protection

Act of 2000—a federal law to protect the victims of trafficking and prosecute their traffickers—defines sex trafficking as the "recruitment, harboring, transportation, provision, or obtaining of a person for the purpose of a commercial sex act, in which the commercial sex act is induced by force, fraud, or coercion, or in which the person induced to perform such act has not attained 18 years of age."[1] A commercial sex act includes any sex act for which anything of value is given to or received by any person.

Without a doubt, this is a growing problem that is traumatizing real people and real lives. While the news and media outlets are exposing parts of the trafficking industry, it takes considering the numbers of sex trafficking to truly get a glimpse into the problem:

- According to the United Nations, sex trafficking worldwide generates more than $150 billion every year, the second largest form of organized crime behind drug trafficking[2]

- In 2013 it was estimated that as many as 27 million people were being trafficked around the world; this includes children, men, and women[3]

- Within forty-eight hours of running away, one out of every three teens will be lured into sex trafficking[4]

- As many as 2.8 million children run away in the United States every year (National Center for Missing and Exploited Children)[5]

As a survivor and now a trained professional in the field, I have been passionately involved in working to effect change by doing prevention and aftercare service work with victims across the nation. The ultimate goal of my own and many others' work is to create a paradigm shift in the way victims are treated and viewed in society, and to prevent trafficking by reducing or eliminating the underlying problems that make youth vulnerable to being trafficked.

For me, this means addressing the problem from the root by exploring what has gone wrong in a child's life that has made him or her exposed to sex trafficking. Usually, I find out that a child has experienced some various forms of abuse, neglect or other trauma. In the United States at present there is a very symptomatic approach to addressing sex trafficking that doesn't take into account outside sources or past issues. Trafficking doesn't happen in a vacuum—it is a symptom of much larger issues that are rarely and only inadequately addressed today. While this book focuses on sex trafficking, it also sheds light on a few of those other issues that are interconnected with the problem.

It's critical that people understand that while sex trafficking is a problem with far-reaching consequences, every individual can all be a part of the solution. As it is now, most would agree that trafficking sounds like a horrible problem but they don't see that it has anything to do with their lives. Even when they learn that it's happening in their own country, they feel that they don't have time to volunteer at a women's shelter or don't live in an inner city where this kind of wrongdoing happens. This book explains why child sex trafficking is an issue that affects us all and describe ways that we can all intervene, whether directly or indirectly.

When the word "intervention" comes up in relation to a child in an abusive situation, most people think it means calling the police or social services. While calling authorities is part of mandatory reporting laws for professionals such as teachers and health care workers, this is not the only type of intervention. Every time you pause to converse with a child about their thoughts and experiences, every time you resist the urge to turn away when faced with a child who is acting out, every time you show compassion for another human being, you are making a difference in that person's life. It's not busting down doors and ripping kids out of trafficking situations. It is far more complicated than that. You cannot rescue anyone, but you can witness, support and love him or her through the bad times as well as the good ones as they go through their experiences of overcoming, seeing relief and feeling joy again.

In this book you'll read about what real intervention looks like and the things you can do in your families and communities. In my own life, these kinds of interactions made a cumulative and positive impact. I believe those positive messages helped me build resiliency and set the foundation for me to be able to overcome my trauma.

I wrote this book to help people in any profession, family, or community role understand the effects of abuse. It is for everyone, from educators to parents, from law enforcement officers to politicians, from teens to adults. There were so many people in my life that had the best of intentions, people who could have and would have helped me if only they had known what to look for. This book helps uncover those hidden signs of trouble, whether in your own child or in another child in your life, and gives you the tools and knowledge needed to make a positive difference in their lives.

> "We live in a world where an abuser can spot a vulnerable child from a mile away, or from across a crowded room, yet every other adult in the child's life is likely to miss it."

My Story

I was one of the luckier ones, at least in the beginning. For the first five years of my life, I had two parents who loved me and took very good care of me. There was little disruption—all my needs were met, and I knew if I cried I would be attended to. It set the foundation for my brain to grow and develop the way it should. I was able to make connections with other people and know that if something happened, someone would take care of me.

My parents tried to do the absolute best they knew how, I know this in my heart. My dad was like a toned down version of Liam Neeson; he wanted to protect me and make sure I knew how to protect myself in any situation. In case anyone tried to grab me or hurt me, he taught me how to find pressure points, how to shoot, and how to take out a grown man using only my little finger.

My mom protected me through education. She taught me that no one was allowed to touch or look at my *private parts* except for the doctor and only when mommy was in the room. Only mommy and daddy were allowed to wash me in the tub. If anything ever felt uncomfortable, I learned I needed to tell them right away.

It was pretty standard teaching and for all intents and purposes they did a great job. It is the exact educational steps I hear repeatedly from parents about protecting kids from sexual abuse and other abuses and trauma. But children do not come with a handbook and even the best of intentions can still fall short.

Despite my parent's best efforts, I was sexually abused. The first time it happened was shortly after my parents separated when I was just six years old. My mom moved from our home in Nevada to live with her sister and husband and their sons in Arizona until she could get on her feet. Not wanting to leave my school, I stayed in Nevada with my dad and visited my mom on school breaks. It was during one of these visits that my life changed forever. One day my mom had to leave for a while to run some errands, leaving my uncle to watch me while she was out. My teenage cousin took full advantage of the opportunity to be alone with me. Instead of a normal afternoon that should have been spent playing outside on the swing set or reading a book in my room, my cousin raped me.

Within a short time after it happened, my uncle walked in and realized that something inappropriate was going on. He gave us both a good stern talking to, and after what seemed like hours of standing against a wall told us that if we promised not to do it again he wouldn't tell my mother, and neither should I.

I didn't tell her and to this day, I am not sure if I would have told her if my uncle hadn't advised me to keep quiet. I would hope that the education about private parts my parents had instilled in me would have made a difference, but I never got the chance to find out.

My behavior changed. I went from always being on task

and engaged at school to being sent to the back of the room. The few friends I had all disappeared. I was highly sexualized and was trying to make sex jokes and even went to the trouble of *stuffing* my shirt to make it appear like I had boobs. I began telling extravagant lies to get attention and started wetting the bed on a regular basis. I became increasingly aggressive toward my parents, but a pushover in situations with other people.

My mom and dad moved forward with the divorce and continued living in different states. I still don't know all of the back-story, the *why* and the *how come*, but I started moving back and forth between their homes. When I lived with my dad I went to the same school but while with my mom, who worked multiple jobs, we moved around a lot. I switched schools often.

Much later in life I learned that the first instance of sexual abuse by my cousin, together with the instability created from moving around so much, made me at risk of having the same thing happen to me again.

So it shouldn't be surprising that I was molested off and on by another family member from the age of seven all the way to age thirteen. My bad behaviors became worse, my grades continued to drop, my personal hygiene became almost nonexistent, and I tried desperately to make people like me at school. But I usually made things worse for myself. I don't remember ever having a childhood *best friend* although there were girls that I believed filled that role, but looking back I realize I made up friendships with them to feel connected and to try fitting in.

Everything was on a downward spiral. I was now spending most of my time living with my mom. Life at her house became unstable after she got into another relationship and my little brother was born. We moved. She worked. We moved over and over, and every time we landed in a new place, I met a new abuser.

It seemed as if someone had crept into my room at night and tattooed "come rape me" on my forehead. In addition, nearly everywhere we went something sexual happened. I spent the years between sixth and eighth grade trying to figure out why I could not attract the guys I liked, but seemed to get assaulted or molested almost everywhere I went.

I started to act out in self-destructive ways. I began cutting, attempting suicide, and dabbling in various illicit drugs. I huffed paint, played the *choking* game, and tried other risky activities I was exposed to by the less than healthy people around me. I pushed the boundaries of everything, yet I still desperately sought to fit in somewhere. School diminished in its importance, leaving me mystified to this day how I passed any of my classes. And I remained confused by the only kind of attention that came my way—the sexual kind.

At the age of 15, I went in and out of a few different relationships. One of them resulted in a move away from my mom's house and into a meth lab. That drug ruled my world. Through a miracle, I was able to get out of that situation and move into a shelter for homeless youth where my daily life improved a lot. I took GED classes, worked full-time, and gained a welcome, yet unfamiliar, sense of independence.

My life was looking up for the first time in a long time when a man down the street invited (well, recruited) me into the seedy world of pornography. Again, this was the theme throughout my life. Every time I took two steps forward, something like that would happen to push me five steps back; each time a little deeper into my addiction, a little more withdrawn from my family, and a little more angry and worthless.

I managed to get out of the pornography world before the photographer went beyond just taking photos of me. I had the sense to run straight back to my mom where I began helping her on her paper route, one of three jobs she had at the time. There I met a woman who was about 10 years older than I was. We hit it off immediately. She became the friend I had always been searching for, and I went everywhere with her, whether it was running silly errands or just hanging out in her room. I attached to her, and while I thought it was because we were close and had a special bond, with my now *adult* eyes, I realize it was because I was so incredibly desperate for love that I didn't want to let her go.

Like many teenagers, I got a fake ID. In my usual quest to push myself to the edge, I longed to be grown up and use that ID at a bar or strip club or somewhere cool. My friend offered to take me to a club—a sex club—where stripping contests and drinking were routine. I was a bit uncomfortable with the idea; however, I felt grown up when I was around her so I thought I could handle it. If anything, we could at least get a good laugh. So I got some money for a sexy, new outfit and headed to the club after work.

There I was, a teenager at a sex club on a Wednesday night—a very late night. I spewed vulnerability. While others in society saw me as a rebellious teen with no boundaries, a high school dropout and drug addict, the man standing outside the club saw me as a vulnerable little girl desperately needing to be loved. He saw me as easy to manipulate despite the hard, brave face I showed to the world.

That night was the game changer. It marked the beginning

of my descent into sex trafficking.

Coincidentally, it was at this exact same time that everyone who was *not* involved in my culture or way of life could have made a difference. Instead, my family, educators, doctors, law enforcement officers, and community members continued viewing me as a *rebellious teen*, not a *vulnerable, hurting girl*. I was the definition of *at-risk youth*.

When I walked out the door of that club that night, the man who would eventually *traffic* me, saw the vulnerable, needy girl with low, nearly non-existent self-esteem that I'd become, and he pounced.

> **Note to everyone:** It is important to realize that not all stories are the same. Trafficking is a very broad topic with moving parts that evolve and unique to each individual's experiences. No snapshot image of trafficking exists, but what is common are the themes. Themes of vulnerability, the tactics of traffickers, and the mindsets of buyers.

I am not going to go into the horrific details that might typically be expected here. I don't think it's helpful for this particular book or subject. Knowing details like how many buyers I would service a day, what my quota was, or when and how I was beaten and by whom does not help us *prevent* trafficking. I have no judgment of the survivors who choose to share these parts of their lives but in this context my goal is to focus on prevention. I want you, and everyone in this world, to shift the mindset of the people in our communities to see these kids the way traffickers see them. I want everyone to see that some people perform behaviors and show tough exteriors for what they are in truth: vulnerabilities. Instead of judging and condemning, rejecting and seeing them as hopeless throwaways, I want you and everyone else to identify the desperate state these people are in and love and support them into and through their process of healing.

I want parents and communities to be watchful for hurting, vulnerable youth and intervene before they go down the slippery path to the eager, open arms of a trafficker.

Over the months as I was trafficked, I was provided with *free* rent in an apartment and was taken out to other homes where I would perform a sex act. After, the money would be given to my trafficker and I would be dropped back at the apartment where I was being held. Then I would go back to the spot reserved for especially for me—on the floor behind the couch—where I was told to stay, where I had to ask permission to use the bathroom, and where I had to beg for food.

I quickly fell into the routine of taking orders, the only communication I experienced during that time. It was much like living the life of a dog with a harsh master.

Eventually I was moved to a massage parlor to work during the same hours my trafficker worked at his nine-to-five job as a security officer. After several months, the massage parlor came under investigation by the police, causing a stir for my trafficker. He and others involved in the scheme caught wind of the investigation because Child Protective Services had contacted the parents of one of the "massage therapists" asking about their child's involvement in a prostitution ring.

Traffickers act quickly once they start to feel the heat. I was asked to leave both the massage parlor and the apartment and come back in a few weeks after things died down. So I went home. My mom was not very happy to see me. In her eyes, I was a run-away and had caused her grief for my months' long absence.

Within a few days, I was back to my old life, hanging out with some of my old crew. As hard as it is to believe now, I didn't tell any of them about what had transpired during my months away from them. It didn't take long to slip back into the familiar patterns of my pre-trafficking life. Within no time at all I started *using* again and began dating a drug dealer who shouldn't have even been looking at someone my age.

Sticking with another familiar pattern of my life, I'd connected with yet another person who didn't really care about me. Eventually, he left me stranded in the middle of the desert in a shed. I'll spare the details, but suffice it to say the police found me three days later. Instead of being rescued, I was immediately arrested on a charge for being a *runaway*, a charge that went back a few years when I was just 14 years old. My mom picked me up. As expected, the experience took her happiness level down another notch.

That's when I went to live with my dad.

After a few weeks with him, an opportunity came up to move from Arizona to California where another one of my uncles and his wife lived. I'd always had a good relationship with my uncle and he did pretty well for himself, so I took the offer seriously. Having nothing to lose, I found myself on the road to California. It wasn't long before I had a job, and I was even following the household rules—a new experience for me. I had new friends who, contrary to my usual friendship choices, didn't get high. I was doing great.

Then, after a night of drinking mixed with a few pills, my aunt, in her own compromised state of mind, sexually assaulted me.

After going through so many bad experiences and managing to clean up and make some good choices, here I was, back in the grip of sexual abuse. Before the assault, I was preparing to attend college and had taken the first steps by studying for my GED. Now it seemed pointless. A friend took my call, picked me up, and took me back home to Arizona.

I suppose it was at this point that I lost hope. I began shooting up meth and transitioned into full-time life on the streets of Phoenix. I lost contact with everyone I knew except for a few select friends. I stopped calling my daddy completely; I stopped dropping by my mom's house, and because I was shooting up, I even stopped talking to the people I used to get high with. I was heading down toward rock bottom. Beyond being *at-risk*, now I was apathetic. I waited for the day to come when I would die from an overdose or get killed over a bad drug deal. I think I probably would have welcomed it at that point.

After about a year on the streets, I got word that my grandmother was in the hospital. Somehow I found my way there, despite the drugs in my system. I hadn't seen most of my family in two years, but I desperately wanted to see my grandma.

When I walked into her hospital room, many of my family members were already there. Their jaws dropped when I walked in. I was all of about 76 pounds (I am 5"4'), had chopped off all of my hair in a fit of rage, and had fresh track marks all over my arms.

The following day a priest came in to read my grandma her last rites. I'd fallen asleep on the other bed in the small room. He started read the last rites to me. He thought I was the one at death's door.

Over the next few days my grandma's health declined

and eventually she was moved to hospice. On the night of her passing, I sat next to her bed. Looking up, I realized I was directly across from the person who started me on my path of destruction—the one who raped me when I was just 6 years old. At the time I didn't think about the irony or the significance of the next few moments, but I was holding my grandma's left hand and my abuser (one of many) was holding her right hand. In the moment it didn't really bother me that he was there. All I kept thinking was what a horrible person I was to have not visited my grandma for a long time and how I was a piece of crap for getting high in the hospital bathroom.

Everyone in the family took time to say their goodbyes, telling her it was okay to let go. When it came to be my turn, I bent over and whispered in her ear, "I'm so sorry I have let you down. I promise I will not get high again." Within moments, she passed away.

I was sick of letting everyone down. I was tired from life on the streets. Being around my family again jolted me back to reality, forcing me to make some decisions. My grandma's death spurred me to try again, to hop back on the horse and make yet another attempt to stay clean. The only problem was that I saw myself as everyone else saw me: a junkie, a runaway, a high school dropout, a loser. Never once did it cross my mind that the abuse I had endured going all the way back to childhood, contributed to my actions.

I stayed with various family members for a couple of weeks. I ate. I slept. I ate and slept. And slept some more. Years of physical and emotional harm had drained me. I was weary to the bone. With some rest, I began to feel pretty good and more productive. I was slowly getting back into good graces with those with whom I had burned bridges. They were gracious and allowed me back into their lives.

I made it two weeks, but the more I was awake and the more I attempted to try to interact with *normal* people, the more I felt that I didn't belong with them. As much as I wanted to stay away from drugs, the mere thought of getting high began its seductive pull. But how and where was I to get drugs or needles? An addict's mind quickly calculates how to get them, which led me to the last place I'd used. Right before visiting my grandma in the hospital I'd left my purse filled with drugs and needles (along with pretty much everything I owned—all of my belongings) with a trusted friend. Now I needed a master plan to find and get my purse back.

Note to Everyone: In our society we have a misconception that the reason people relapse is because they are addicted to the feeling they get from using drugs. There is no doubt some drugs provide the user with a momentary, fleeting good feeling. And, of course, there are issues with physical addictions and withdrawals that make it very difficult to quit. However, at the core, there is no difference between being addicted to heroin or addicted to gambling, apart from the addiction cultures and the associated dangers. Addictions are a way for us to zone out, to avoid being part of a world we can't emotionally handle. Obviously, using drugs is more dangerous in many ways than being addicted to online shopping, gambling or other seemingly harmless addictions, but at their core they are all the same. They are a way to escape. Drugs are just more stigmatized than other addictions and they impact a person's physical health in ways that gambling and shopping do not.

I needed to get my purse back. As I formulated my get-my-purse-back-now plan, opportunity walked right into the room where I was staying at one of my cousin's houses. My cousin's brother-in-law, Tim, walked out of his bedroom on his way to attend class at one of the local community colleges. There it was! He would be my out. He told me he was heading out to art class, which was only a five-minute drive from my purse. I knew exactly what to say to get him to give me a ride. I told him how much I envied that he had such a strong purpose for his life, and that I wished I knew what that felt like. Though in some ways I believe I meant those words, my focus was purely on getting to that purse any way I could.

I hadn't done anything normal in years, so it wasn't surprising that my 80-pound body was clothed in a floral shirt, a size double zero pair of striped dress pants, and a pair of borrowed bowling shoes that were fully two sizes too big, and no socks that day. This was the outfit I wore to my grandma's funeral. I certainly didn't feel abnormal dressed this way but I must have looked a sight to everyone around me.

On the way to get my purse, Tim and I chatted nonchalantly about small details of our lives. Somewhere in that conversation, he mentioned a friend who had done something special for his four-year-old daughter. It happens that she had a hard time growing hair, so her dad completely shaved all of his hair off to help his little girl feel special and not so different. I remember thinking how incredibly loving that act was and what a lasting impression it would surely make in that little girl's life.

We chatted more on the ride. He parked and took me into the school and straight into his art class. I learned how to spray paint that day. Something normal in my not so normal world.

A momentary delay in my quest to get my purse, but a fun one nonetheless.

After class, while driving to my friend's house to get my purse, Tim suggested that if I liked painting I could help him with a painting project he was working on for a store. I'd enjoyed the painting class so I agreed to help, all the while thinking that I would do anything, including painting, to get him to take me back to my purse. I had hoped we would go straight to get my purse, but we diverted to the store instead to buy paint for the project.

Having no other viable options, I went along with it and followed him into the store. The first person I noticed inside was an extremely attractive man sitting on a table. Hmmm, this could be interesting. We were introduced. As it turned out, this handsome man before me was the mostly bald friend with the little girl who couldn't grow hair. We hit it off immediately! Without even a hint of awkwardness or shyness, we started sharing tidbits about our lives. Before I knew it, I was sharing with him everything that I had needed to say for a long time but didn't know how with anyone else. He listened to me, encouraged me and shared his own addiction-riddled past.

That night when it was time to leave, I felt like I was madly in love. Looking back, it was part of my pattern of glowing when a friend or someone, anyone, paid even a bit of attention to me.

As Tim and I prepared to leave the store, I decided this guy was someone I wanted to see again and hopefully have in my life in some way. We exchanged numbers. Wouldn't you know, in the glow of the evening's conversation, I completely forgot about my purse, not even thinking about it until much later after returning to my cousin's house.

Note to Survivors: This sounds like the beginning of a love story, but in actuality I was putting myself in yet another very vulnerable position. Someone could have very easily sensed my vulnerable state and taken advantage of it. I had only been clean a few weeks. I had a significant trauma history. I had no place to call home. I was only 18 and this could have easily ended in another abusive relationship.

After waking the following morning, I couldn't contain the urge to call my newfound friend. I'd been awake most of the night thinking about him and our lively conversation. It was Halloween morning 2003. Even though I was filled with anxiety by the thought that he wouldn't want to hear from me again because he probably viewed me as a messed up, used up girl—a failure—I dialed his number anyway. It's an understatement to say I was in shock when he said he wanted to see me again and he wanted to invite me to come trick-or-treating with him and his little girl that night!

We couldn't get enough of each other, and ended up talking throughout the morning and on into the afternoon. When he pulled up in his car to pick up for trick-or-treating, I was pleasantly surprised to see that he wasn't alone. His little girl was also in the car, sitting quietly in the back seat, dressed like Dorothy from "The Wizard of Oz," complete with long braids, a little basket carrying Toto, and sparkling ruby red slippers. Overwhelmed with emotion, I hugged him and then heard a little voice blurt out from the back seat in the cutest voice ever: "My daddy thinks you are pretty."

In our long conversation just 24 hours earlier, he told me

that I needed something outside of myself to get out of my self-destructive cycle. In that moment I wanted nothing more than for it to be them.

Road to Recovery

I went home with him that night. I never looked back and 12 years later we are still together. Even though my relationship was and is successful, there are still a few things to unpack here. I want to start by saying I am in a great relationship, but not a perfect one—that doesn't exist. This relationship is not abusive and that is what is important. We both love each other deeply. My husband could have been another abuser, but he wasn't. Instead of preying on my vulnerabilities, he loved and supported me for exactly who I was and where I was at that moment. He also believed in me when everyone else had stopped. This was key, and hopefully as the book unfolds you will see how incredibly important that is for the healing process.

My husband in no way saved me. I don't believe that he did and neither does he. People have publicly thanked him for "doing a good job with his wife," but at the end of the day I have done the hard work to overcome my past, get my education, and develop my career. I was able to do it when I did because I made the choice to get out and move into a loving, supportive environment. Together, my husband and I have broken a generational cycle of abuse. The ideology that other people are responsible for someone's success, such as overcoming their past, is wrong. While it certainly helped that my husband had overcome his own time on the streets and his own addictions and was able to share his story with me, I was the one who made the choice to change my life. More on that later.

I wish I could say that after meeting my husband, everything was rainbows and sunshine, and the past was in the past. Life was better. I'd made it through the valleys and the shadows. I went from being on the streets and having nothing and no one to having a husband, four amazing kids, a house, a car, and heavy involvement in the community. Yes, it was an improvement. My life was exponentially different from the past. I volunteered in the classroom and shuttled kids to dance classes and cheerleading practice. I was given baby showers and planned birthday parties. I lived in the suburbs, miles away from any of the people I'd used drugs with and the places I'd been trafficked. My husband worked and I took care of the kids. We struggled financially but as the American dream goes, we'd "made it." For me, this equated to being healed; I felt like I should have peace in my life because I was no longer on the streets or using.

But after giving birth to our first baby and our sweet older girl turning six, things started to go downhill fast. My anxiety increased and I started having insomnia. I'd made it through my first year clean—an incredible accomplishment—and thought things would get better, but instead, they seemed to get worse. One thing that was certain; I wanted to give my kids a better life than my own. I figured I was doing better than my parents because my kids weren't being sexually abused. They had stability and they came from an intact family with two parents who were involved in their lives. However, as time went on, things got worse. I had another baby and started to unravel a bit. Some online research introduced me to postpartum depression. I read self-help books and began taking Zoloft, a prescription drug intended to treat my depression. I began feeling a little better but then I became pregnant again and things quickly went downhill.

I knew I needed help, so I made an appointment with an agency that provided counseling. It didn't take a mental health practitioner long to assess and quickly diagnose me with bipolar disorder and put me on a psych medication. It seemed to be an answer in an answerless situation. I felt somewhat numb to the world, but for the most part I was still anxious and overwhelmed. Relying on gut instinct, I took a chance on another mental health practitioner, went through another assessment, received a new diagnosis and new pill, and was referred to group therapy. I tried group therapy, but it didn't really connect, so I started reading more online and made sure I stayed up on my medications. Not one to give up, I tried again, got another agency, another assessment, a third and different diagnosis, and another medication. The drugs—this time the legal kind—caused me to be completely out of it most of the day. Feeling like I was in a haze, my ability to take care of my kids was hindered. After a series of close calls, I stopped taking all of the medications so that I could try and fix myself.

Note to Service Providers: It's significant to understand that during this time I went through many assessments from a variety of mental health professionals at various levels of education and experience. Not one of them asked me if I had experienced abuse or trauma. I will never know if I would have revealed my trauma history at that point because I still did not recognize the events from my days being trafficked as abuse or trauma. However, it should have been asked by every mental health professional. It is so important to ask and look for signs of abuse before trying to help others. Without taking these steps, the people you help can easily be misdiagnosed and progress delayed.

Over the years I had difficulty completing assignments and tasks. My brain constantly raced from one thought to the next. I'd started school but dropped out and felt like I was never going to get my GED. My husband kept telling me to just go take it to see if I could pass it without studying. If I failed parts of the test, I could take them after studying those specific areas. I was tired of hearing myself *saying* I was going to study, so I gathered the courage to step out of my pattern and take the test. Filled with anxiety over fear of failure, I convinced myself that I would fail the entire test. Much to my surprise, I passed every section! That one accomplishment gave me enough confidence that I enrolled in community college. I was 24 years old with four kids, and even though going to college scared me, I'd discovered a love for photography and wanted to take it to the next step. I enrolled in photography classes with the intent of getting a fifteen-credit photography certificate.

Right around the time I started college I inadvertently stumbled across the terminology of *sexual slavery* while looking through Facebook posts. Curious, I did a little more research and called an organization that dealt with this topic and spoke with the man on the other end of the phone about my past. In that conversation, three key things took place that made it a life-changing experience:

First, I came to the realization that I was in a safe environment where I had food in my belly, a roof over my head, felt loved, and had gained some independence.

Second, for the first time I recognized that I had been a victim of something pretty awful and there was a name for it: *sexual slavery.*

Third, I was listened to by the man on the phone; he did

not judge me and he reassured me that none of it was my fault.

Even though I had absolutely no idea at the time that something special and transforming had transpired and I didn't yet understand these concepts, it was this list that fundamentally changed my life and built a foundation for me to begin healing.

If we can recreate these scenarios in our community, we will be much more effective with interventions.

Shortly after that conversation, I was put in contact with a therapist who had created a trauma-informed curriculum and worked as trauma-therapist for 17 years. She was working on a project to create a healing curriculum specifically for victims of commercial sexual exploitation. We started working together. As time passed, I began to understand the effects of trauma in my life. In the process, the curriculum took shape and has since been used to help many others in my situation.

Within a year of starting in trauma treatment, the diagnosis I'd received, complex PTSD (Post-Traumatic Stress Disorder) was 90 percent gone. In later chapters I will go into more detail about events that transpired and why it is so important to take a trauma approach when working with vulnerable populations of any kind. But as testament to my healing and how far I have come the past five years, this one statistic more than any other cements it in place. Nowhere is the healing more evident than the geographical location from which I spend my days working to help others prevent trauma and abuse through community education. Our office is right across the street from the location where I was trafficked.

I completed my first semester of college with a 4.0 GPA and received a full ride scholarship to our local community college. As is the case with many college students, I changed majors once or twice, eventually gravitating to the school of social work—another good decision. After completing my associate's degree, I received a full scholarship to attend Arizona State University to get a bachelor's degree. I graduated with a Bachelor of Social Work with a minor in Women and Gender Studies. You can imagine the excitement in our household on graduation day!

Over the past five years, I have worked in the field to provide community education and encourage collaboration among local and national organizations. I am a dedicated advocate for understanding and implementing trauma-informed care practices and approaches for various populations.

Ending commercial sexual exploitation is my life's work and as a survivor I hope I can impact others to use a trauma-informed approach to help support, love, and empower vulnerable populations.

There are so many factors that contribute to trafficking and sexual slavery—demand, race, class, and gender inequality—all needing to be addressed to make a difference. In this book, I focus on the types of trauma that make children vulnerable, the array of experiences that need to be addressed in our society, and how everyone—parents, grandparents, teachers, social workers, counselors, coaches, Girl Scout leaders, neighbors, Sunday School teachers—can do their part to prevent our youth from the trajectory of abuse into sex trafficking, and identify and intervene when we spot it.

CHAPTER 1

What Exactly Is Sex Trafficking?

I did not understand what *sex trafficking* meant until I was well into my twenties, despite the fact that I had experienced and lived it. I knew that I'd been sexually abused as a child, but never once did I tie it to my slide into sex trafficking.

The more I work in this field, the more I realize how common this misunderstanding is among those who have been trafficked. As I provide seminars and workshops on sex trafficking, trauma, and abuse to mental health professionals, service providers, parents, teachers, and others, at least one person and sometimes several people privately disclose their own sexual abuse or other trauma after they've listened to my story and absorbed this new information. Often, it is the first time they've ever uttered the words out loud about their less-than-normal experiences. It's a great first step and it's the reason I love doing what I do.

What I did not expect is that there is a pattern of individuals who volunteer for sex trafficking prevention organizations who realize only after they've become volunteers that they were sexually abused and are also survivors. I've heard this story so often that I expect it. I have met and worked with many people who became involved through school or volunteer organizations but did not recognize themselves as survivors because they didn't fit the definition of trafficking portrayed in the media. They were not a young girl kidnapped from a mall or outside their home by complete strangers and then beaten, raped, and drugged into submission, so they were in the dark about their own abuse victim status. This has not only caused problems in our communities by showing a very small slice of the reality and magnitude of trafficking, but also makes it very hard for survivors to connect with the stories, which then perpetuates victims feeling like it is their fault if they don't meet those minimum requirements.

I think it is incredibly important to talk about the many forms of exploitation to get a broad picture of how it can happen in our society. This chapter is an overview of trafficking with some basic definitions, but if this is the first time you are being introduced to the topic, I would highly suggest reading Rachel Lloyd's *"Girls Like Us"* or Holly Smith's *"Walking Prey"*. Both are amazing survivor leaders who give a survivor-informed perspective that is true to what trafficking really is in community.

Defining Trafficking

The federal Trafficking Victims Protection Act defines the crime of human trafficking as:

"**A.** The recruitment, harboring, transportation, provision, or obtaining of a person for the purpose of a commercial sex act where such an act is induced by force, fraud, or coercion, or in which the person induced to perform such act has not attained 18 years of age, or

"**B.** The recruitment, harboring, transportation, provision, or obtaining of a person for labor or services, through the use of force, fraud, or coercion for the purpose of subjection to involuntary servitude, peonage, debt bondage, or slavery."[1]

Many times, because individuals are not neck deep in anti-trafficking efforts, this definition is full of jargon and sounds like second year law school terms. These are important definitions, but the reality is that most cannot relate to the way they are written. They are also not the definitions, explanations or words we would use when working with a survivor, as it would immediately cause further isolation. To be clear, the term trafficking is not used on the streets or by those being exploited.

I think it is important to talk about what trafficking is and how each person perceives it. Bottom line, human trafficking is the exploitation of any human being. It can be in the form of taking advantage of a person who is living in poverty by promising them a better life and then using them for labor to make a profit. It could be a vulnerable housewife whose husband coerces her to have sex with other men at local casino hotels, asking for a few dollars so they can go gambling. Or it could be a 14-year-old girl who has run away from home and ends up having sex with adult men for food and to get her basic survival needs met.

Under the federal Trafficking Victims Protection Act, children under the age of 18 are included as victims of human trafficking; however, this has been misinterpreted to mean that a pimp or trafficker is involved when it actually means any child who is used for sex in any situation that involves trading something of value.

The government developed laws that give us the definition

of human trafficking. It states that it is against the law ". . . if the person induced to perform such act has not attained 18 years of age." While most think that this means there needs to be a pimp or trafficker involved, it actually means any child who is being used for sex in any situation that involves trading something of value.I am not going to go too much into laws and those aspects of trafficking, but I will discuss the mental aspects of exploitation. In the media, the most common portrayal of trafficking is of a young, white girl being kidnapped right from the street in a very similar way to the movie "*Taken*" where an American girl traveling to Paris gets caught up in a ruse by professional traffickers who kidnap young women and sell them as sex slaves.

When I first started doing interviews with the media after my recovery, they wanted the gory, salacious, horrific details to perpetrate this stereotype and push me off as the "all American girl" persona. It is these consistently flawed images reflected in the media that give parents and professionals a skewed and incorrect perspective. It gives potential victims and survivors the false idea that they were not abused.

What does a person who is trafficked look like? Where do they come from? How do they end up there?

Slide into Trafficking

Childhood sexual abuse

I once mentored Sam, a 14-year-old girl. Sam had been raped by her uncle for many years. Her life at home wasn't great, and now with the added trauma, her transition into adolescence wasn't easy. Her grades started dropping. She began to self-harm as a coping mechanism and began running away from home, only to come back when she hit dead ends. Her mom was preoccupied with a series of boyfriends and days and nights filled with drug use. Sam ran away three or four times, staying with friends whose moms took pity on her because they knew her home life wasn't great. These visits usually didn't last long, even though the welcome mat was out and the invitation to stay was open-ended. She always felt like she was too much of a burden on the family, so she would pack her bag and slip away, usually within 24 hours or so. She felt as if there was nowhere to go. In fear of being attacked in her sleep on long nights on the streets, she forced herself to stay awake and walk around until morning light. One fateful night, around 2 am, after two days without food and dazed from sleepless nights, a man pulled up in his car and asked if she was okay and if she'd like a ride. A pivotal moment. She was vulnerable. Exposed. Hungry. Tired. The man offered this hungry, tired, traumatized young girl food for her belly and enough money for a hotel room if she would give him sex or oral sex. Sex wasn't foreign to her. Remember her uncle? As awful her childhood sexual abuse was, it made sex familiar and it made it one step easier to slide into being trafficked. This was Sam's introduction to the horrible life of trafficking. Yet, many would call this prostitution and call her a prostitute. Again, like the law says, a child *cannot* engage in prostitution, ever. It is always considered commercial sexual exploitation of children.

Bands of temporary brothers and sisters

On the streets of a most big cities, you will find groups of six or seven homeless teens work together to protect each other by stealing, selling sex, or panhandling (asking strangers for money in a public place). Their system of group support and collective effort helps them survive. Although they don't work with a pimp, they contribute to the group because it is the only family they have on the streets, and it gets them through to the next day. Most have stories similar to Sam's. Broken homes and distracted parents. Abuse, sexual or other, or other trauma that lead them to seek ways to survive and numb the pain. We see them as miscreants, vandals, juvenile delinquents, or hoodlums. Yet, they end up just as exposed and vulnerable to trafficking as Sam. They're all victims. They are underage children who have no other options. When you're out of options, you sell what you have to the wolves who have money.

Presence of domestic violence

A 30-year-old woman stayed with her boyfriend for several years even though domestic violence was a common component of their relationship, especially when alcohol was involved. After losing her job, finances were tight in their household making the job search a priority. Her boyfriend jokingly suggested that she could make it up by posting sex ads online. She shrugged it off and went back to the job search. The next day during a spate of drinking, he brought it up again. Thinking he wasn't serious, she ignored him. Sadly, he wasn't joking. He erupted into a rage, yelling at her, hitting her, and threw her outside. He told her she could come home once she had $1,000 to contribute to the household. A pivotal moment.

Incest

A young boy who had known only a hard life up to age seven, was introduced to trauma at that tender young age when his father began molesting him. Before long, his father invited other people to their home to also molest his son. At first it was men from the neighborhood, but greed took over once his father realized how profitable online selling could be. His mom turned a blind eye for a time, but she too succumbed to the lure of money and began using her son as trade to supplement her prescription drug addiction. All pivotal moments.

Traffic inside the Border

These are just a few examples of the slide into trafficking and exploitation within our borders. These aren't people who were kidnapped by unscrupulous international sex traffickers. Trafficking truly has no borders; it is simply the use of another human being's body for labor or sex for another human being's monetary or emotional satisfaction. Trafficking preys on the vulnerable through force or manipulation.

Many people believe that at some point, much like with domestic violence, the victim has a choice. That there comes a point when the abuse becomes the victim's *responsibility*. Many think, "Okay, we came and picked you up nine times and let you sleep at our house and have a homemade meal and took you to church. Now it's your turn to fix yourself," or "You are almost 18 years old; it's time you start taking care of yourself and making your own decisions," or "You are 50 years old now. I understand it started when you were 13 but you're grown up and you have no excuses anymore. You must still want to be out there."

The quantity of trauma that a person endures while in the *life* (a commonly used term by survivors and sex workers to refer to being involved in prostitution or in the *game*) can't be turned off like the dripping of a faucet. Many view themselves as prostitutes or hookers, and even though the truth is that they are sex slaves and they honestly want out, they cannot and do see themselves through the same lens that we see them. They cannot get out without outside intervention. In my time working to help victims of sex trafficking, I have never had a young kid run up to me screaming, "Please help! I am a victim of sex trafficking and my trafficker is right behind me! Call the national human trafficking hotline!" Instead, what I see is a 13-year-old being picked up on shoplifting charges, who won't talk because her pimp has trained her not to speak to anyone about anything and that he will be there to pick her from jail and bail her out. I see a 15-year-old who is in shelter, glamorizing the *life* and using terms like, "I've been *ho-ing* since I was 13 and it's how I make my money," or "It's my life and I am in control." This is not because this person is a *bad* kid. It does not make them any less of a victim. It is the result of manipulation and living in survival mode from extensive compounded trauma throughout their lives.

If we really want to help our youth, our neighbors, our families, we need to start talking about this realistically; not the way it is portrayed in the media. In all of these cases, not one single person identified themselves as victims of sex slavery or human trafficking. They had been led to believe by larger society that it doesn't happen within our borders, in our homes, and on our streets. Unknown to them, they were living the true definition of sex trafficking without even knowing it.

These pages could be filled with example after example, story after story, but barely scratch the surface of all the ways children and adults are exploited. I hope I have painted a picture for you that it is broader than what you may have seen in the media or from a basic trafficking presentation at school or church.

While it's true that the scenario of three white teenage girls being targeted at the mall by a trafficker posing as a modeling agent comports with the definition of trafficking, statistics show that it is more likely that young women of color, LGBTQ, or homeless youth, intersected with poverty, who are at the highest risk. With the middle class disappearing and poverty increasing, we are bound to see an increase in trafficking. But we shouldn't assume that affluence or color immunizes against trafficking. Sexual abuse and adverse childhood experiences span across racial, socioeconomic, gender and other divides. With the ease of access to porn that's broadcast right through our phones, iPads, and computer screens, the net is wider and the vulnerable population increases.

Ignoring these realities will not bring victims the hope and freedom that they deserve and will instead perpetuate cycles that make it even harder for them to get out and stay out.

Getting Out

What does it mean to get out? Honestly, that topic alone could fill the pages of an entire book. For now, the focus is on the most common question: "Why don't they run?"

More often than not, the question is said with a tinge of contempt or even judgment. Sometimes it's said with empathy and concern, but the questions most heard are rude and focus more on blaming than on helping. "Why didn't you run? or "Where were your parents?" Like I said before, as much as my own parents worked hard to protect me, there were many other factors that contributed to my victimization. Many think that because I had supportive people in my life, I could have never experienced years of sexual abuse and trauma, but I did. I was still vulnerable. There were pivotal moments.

So why don't they run? In a sense, some bond to their trafficker/abuser—a trauma bond. Patrick Carnes, PhD, developed the concept of trauma bonding to describe the misuse of fear, excitement, sexual feelings, and sexual physiology to entangle another person.[2] A trauma bond forms when the victim adapts their mindset to accept the situation they're in.

I was very lucky that I didn't trauma bond to the man who trafficked me. For some reason, I was spared from bonding to him, or having emotional ties to him. I did not see him as my boyfriend, but so many of the other young people I have worked with do. When I was able to leave, I never felt like I needed to run back to him. More than likely this was because I hadn't clung onto or attached to him. For many, the trafficker is the first and sometimes only stable, or stable-seeming, person in their lives. The natural human response is to latch on.

I remember one day when I was able to get away from my trafficker for a few hours. After making it to my friend's house, I yearned to pour my heart out and tell them I needed help, but I was terrified that somehow my trafficker could hear me or that someone was following me to make sure I didn't say anything.

Even though I didn't trauma bond with my trafficker, I did live in fear. I was afraid that he would find me and hurt me if I told anyone or didn't return. I lived in fear of the future: what I would do and where I would go. I had done things, seen things that no child should, and my only instinct was to get through to the next day. Many survivors tell me a similar story; they don't feel like they have the resources to get out because they feel so broken and that they wouldn't fit in anywhere else. They simply believe they can never leave.

Trafficking and Prostitution

If you take everything I have described into account, you might begin to see a piece of just how much is involved in the trafficking industry and how broad this topic is. When we take traumatized people, kids or adults, with very few if any social and familial supports, add in the social shame that comes along with being considered a prostitute or slut, and then compound it by treating the victims as criminals, we give the buyers excuses to come back and traffickers more reason to do business. The economy of trafficking.

There is a lot of work to be done.

This section is from my own experiences and not derived from structured research. I have worked in a professional capacity as a social worker and mentor with many females, males, and non-binary individuals from a broad age range who are contemplating leaving the streets. Every single individual I have worked with experienced exploitation before their 18th birthday, and all but two experienced sexual abuse as children, and the two that did not experience sexual abuse had significant instances of childhood trauma.

This means that at some point, these exploited individuals under federal law would have been considered trafficking victims, but are instead viewed as whores who don't deserve support or empowerment. They are jailed and in most cases treated like the lowest of criminals by law enforcement officers. (Not all; I have worked with some phenomenal law enforcement officers who were victim-focused with a caring and compassionate perspective). Then the victims are charged with prostitution a misdemeanor for the first arrest in most states. After a few more arrests, the misdemeanors turn into felony charges.

The buyer on the other hand are usually required to take eight hours of "John's school", which is similar to an 8-hour defensive driving class. In it they are lectured on why it's bad to buy sex. Not the most effective training. The idea behind the school is good, but content needs improvement.

Healthy vs. Unhealthy Sex

People involved in sex work have the highest homicide rates because it is not about consensual sex but instead about power and control. They are treated like property. Common among buyers of sex is the belief that when a buyer is paying for an individual's body for a certain amount of time, that person owns them for those 20 minutes or that hour.

I support sex positivism and people being able to engage in whatever kind of sex they want, as long as it is consenting and there is no coercion or manipulation involved. The problem is that our society trains us to see woman as sex objects to be used for the sole pleasure of a man. Although we've made a few big steps toward equality between the genders, this dangerous view not only stands as barrier to progress, but also gives buyers an excuse to abuse women.

Controversy abounds around the topic of adults engaging in sex work. One of the main debates is whether or not legalizing prostitution would help the issue or cause more harm. Countless examples and arguments are used about the successful legalization of prostitution in other countries, and even countries where prostitution is illegal but instead of the victims getting arrested, the buyers get the harsh punishments and the victims go free. For me, there is no denying the fact that engaging in sex work can be highly risky, even with safeguards put in place. This is not the fault of the individual but is due to the much larger issues of privilege and violence against minorities. One of the most appealing arguments for legalization is creating safer environments for engagement, as well as dropping felony charges if an individual chooses to exit sex work. This would allow the victim to leave without shame and without a record that will haunt him or her for the rest of his or her life.

My main concern with the legalization argument is that pornography is legal and available literally at your fingertips; you can get it anywhere. Yet, child pornography is not legal and is still mass produced and viewed in every part of the world. Having legal adult pornography does not curb the thirst of those who seek child porn. Legalizing adult sex work will also not curb buying sex with children.

In the end, simplifying the solution of trafficking to legalizing or not legalizing is an arduous and preposterous task. It's never been that simple nor will it ever be. It is an issue of race, class, and gender inequalities. It is an issue of rampant and unresolved generational abuse and trauma. It is an issue of violence and entitlement to another human being's body. It is correcting the flawed perception that one human life means more than another's. It is about the of lack education around trauma and abuse. It is about equipping community leaders, parents, and professionals with the tools and support to create cultural change within communities and institutions.

The incidence of sex trafficking, both in the U.S. and abroad, has been called into question in recent times. Claims are made that the numbers are a farce; that trafficking in the States and around the globe doesn't exist in the numbers claimed by the statistics.

The reality is that this is not a new issue. The numbers that we do have don't begin to scratch the surface. This is mostly because of the lack of the public's awareness and the lack of identification of victims. We know this because of the reports from organizations that work with vulnerable populations—poverty, homelessness, child abuse, and others—who believe they don't have any trafficking victims in their case load, and at the same time admit to having worked with a dozen or so child prostitutes in the space of a year. Or they can remember one instance such as helping a 13-year-old boy who traded sex for drugs. We know the lack of awareness is real because there is such a huge disconnect in the language used to identify trafficking victims. In the end, it makes numbers harder to track and report.

Whether the numbers show the actual extent of trafficking or not, it is crucial that we understand the realities and do something about them. We cannot deny the statistics that measure the brutality and trauma that individuals experience while being trafficked. The average time a person is commercially exploited is seven years after the first exploitation. If a child is forced into the sex trade at the age of 13, life expectancy is 20 years, mostly due to violence perpetrated against them, which leads victims to drug overdoses, suicides, and untreated sexual diseases.[3]

Prevention of trafficking is more than educating junior high and high school kids. Prevention is learning to recognize the signs of trafficking that are already occurring. It is about recognizing vulnerable children before a trafficker does.

Trafficking is the symptom of larger social issues, and in order to address a symptom, we cannot simply put a Band-Aid on it. We must address it from the root. By understanding the issues that contribute to trafficking, we can aid in the beginning; in preventing and creating the paradigm shift needed to effectively address and combat it. We have a long way to go and a lot of work to do, but collectively, the work and voices will make a difference.

Moving forward, it is important to note that this book is not all about trafficking—it is about addressing the major causes. I hope this first chapter gave you an overview of the problem. The remaining chapters will focus on addressing the roots of the issue.

CHAPTER 2

How and Why Trafficking Happens

Trauma shakes us to the core. Regardless of what kind of trauma it is—seeing your parents fight to not having enough food; a car accident to being trafficked—trauma interrupts normal development and forces us into survival mode. Hearts racing, minds hindered, we do our best to respond to abnormal situations in a normal way just get through the crisis and on to the next minute, hour or day.

How do we know that trauma has occurred? Especially when we don't have a good grasp of all that trauma encompasses. A large study was conducted by Centers for Disease Control and Prevention and Kaiser Permanente's Health Appraisal Clinic in San Diego to understand associations between childhood maltreatment and later-life health and well-being.[1] From that study came the ACE (Adverse Childhood Experiences) questionnaire, a simple, straight-forward ten-question assessment used to measure trauma and compounded trauma (one trauma layered on top of another) resulting from adverse childhood experiences.[2] Used to gauge whether a person has experienced trauma, and in what form, events such as sexual abuse, not having enough food or proper living conditions among others, reveals one's trauma history. One point is given for each adverse childhood experience. Once the score is tabulated on a scale of zero to ten, the result indicates the likelihood of suicide, drug or alcohol abuse, and other self-harm risks. An ACE score of zero, for example, indicates a one in 96 likelihood of attempting suicide. A score of one to three significantly increases to one in 10. Four or higher increases that likelihood to one in 5.

Likewise, an ACE score of zero indicates a low likelihood of intravenous drug use, one in 480, but with an ACE score from one to three, the odds go to one in 43. The test provides a revealing glimpse into one's trauma history and fills in the blanks about a life that's taken a few wrong turns, many ending in tragedy and loss.

Trauma left untreated can affect the individual and ultimately impact society at large. In fact, the ACE study revealed many possible outcomes resulting from untreated trauma:

- Inability to hold a job
- Unintended pregnancies
- Problems paying attention
- Relationship issues
- Smoking, alcoholism and drug abuse
- Bullying
- Separation and divorce
- Self-harm
- Severe depression
- Eating disorders
- Health problems (ranging from heart disease to chronic pain)

Getting to the Root

On any given day you might see half a dozen or more campaigns or service messages distributed by non-profits and other well-meaning organizations urging the American public to bring an end to negative social issues like bullying, drug and alcohol addiction, smoking, teen pregnancy, sexually transmitted diseases, human trafficking, domestic violence, coercive control and the list goes on and on.

We tell parents how to parent. We tell kids how to be kids. We pass laws requiring schools to teach Internet safety, and we debate whether sex education should be allowed in schools, and if so, in what form. It doesn't stop there. We tell people how to date, what healthy relationships look like, how to budget, how to quit smoking, and how to kick addictions.

Yet, although most of the prescribed solutions focus on the anticipated result, many fail to focus on the root causes of the issues. They stop short of looking beneath the surface in order to connect the dots from the underlying trauma events leading up to debilitating and tragic outcomes. In this way we expect achievement and success absent deep exploration and release of old wounds. It's like a kitchen faucet with low water pressure. No matter how far you push the handles or even go as far as replacing the hardware, the water pressure remains the same until you look in the cabinet under the sink to find the crack in the water pipe.

What has the ACE Study taught us? We are good at putting the cart before the horse with solution-focused programs. Again, they are well-intentioned, but lacking full information.

Considering that nearly 35 million children[3] have experienced trauma and carry it into their adult lives, all of these negative social issues are caused by a similar root and therefore require a similar solution: addressing the trauma.

Peeling Back the Lid

In many situations, people who experience abuse or grow up in highly toxic homes don't realize that their childhood trauma places them in survival mode, producing toxic stress (produced from living in poverty or working in an abusive environment) that that can and will affect their lives in ways that may not be clear to them. When you think about people who just can't seem to get it together, those who hop from job to job or relationship to relationship, or addicts and run-aways, you are likely seeing trauma.

It's not uncommon for trauma survivors to think that because they are doing better than someone from the previous generation—parents, grandparents or others—that they are okay. Or because they haven't abused their kids or don't act like their abuser did, they are just fine. They fail to recognize that the negative issues that have crept into their lives—multiple divorces, depression, suicidal thoughts, addictions (not just drugs), anxiety—are related to past traumas. We've witnessed a surge of rallying and support in today's young people, and in decades past, behind causes meant to cure negative social issues, but the truth is that unless we help survivors of trauma recognize and connect the dots from past trauma to their current condition, and give them the love and support they deserve, no amount of fundraising, teaching or lecturing them will stop the negative outcomes.

There's little doubt that the ACE Study could have added another 101 items to the trauma effect list, but the bottom line is that dealing with deep roots of trauma, instead of topically addressing the wounds, would alleviate so much of what we spend money and time trying to address. The same study indicated that teenage boys who have an ACE score of four or higher are 76 percent more likely to get a girl pregnant during high school, and yet the majority of our resources tend to focus on abstinence education instead of addressing why teens are at higher risk of pregnancy after experiencing trauma and toxic stress. These adverse childhood experiences not only explain why negative social issues permeate our society, but also why some people experience a dealing in their physical health. Evidence shows that untreated childhood trauma can lead to lifelong physical, mental, emotional and behavioral problems.[4] Imagine the decreases in costs for healthcare, mental health treatment, law enforcement, courts and prisons if we could prevent the trauma from happening in the first place and identify and quickly treat it when it does.

The Trauma Reveal

An interesting phenomenon happens to most people while taking the ACE survey. First, it identifies whether the test-taker has experienced trauma; and second, for those who have, it begins to build a foundation of understanding about the source of lifelong problems. One simple test that takes less than a minute to complete has the effect of revealing the hurt and pain of trauma that leads to self-sabotage or destruction. It clears the fog and gives hope to evaporate the almost always present shame.

Before moving forward, please take a moment to take the ACE test for yourself. It's not scary. In fact, you may be surprised. If you are a professional who works with abuse, violence, abuse or other social issues, taking this test yourself will open your eyes to a new way of viewing yourself and how you can better help others. You can either write your answers and score in the book or keep track on a separate sheet of paper.

The Adverse Childhood Experience Test
Reprinted with permission from Vincent J. Felitti, MD

What's My ACE Score?
Prior to your 18th birthday:

1. Did a parent or other adult in the household often or very often…
    * Swear at you, insult you, put you down, or humiliate you? or
    * Act in a way that made you afraid that you might be physically hurt?   If yes, enter 1 _____

2. Did a parent or other adult in the household often or very often…
    * Push, grab, slap, or throw something at you? or
    * Ever hit you so hard that you had marks or were injured?   If yes, enter 1 _____

3. Did an adult or person at least 5 years older than you ever…
    * Touch or fondle you or have you touch their body in a sexual way? or
    * Attempt or actually have oral, anal, or vaginal intercourse with you?   If yes, enter 1 _____

4. Did you often or very often feel that …
    * No one in your family loved you or thought you were important or special? or
    * Your family didn't look out for each other, feel close to each other, or support each other?
          If yes, enter 1 _____

5. Did you often or very often feel that ...
   - You didn't have enough to eat, had to wear dirty clothes, and had no one to protect you? or
   - Your parents were too drunk or high to take care of you or take you to the doctor if you needed it?

   If yes, enter 1 _____

6. Was a biological parent ever lost to you through divorce, abandonment, or other reason?   If yes, enter 1 _____

7. Was your mother or stepmother:
   - Often or very often pushed, grabbed, slapped, or had something thrown at her? or
   - Sometimes, often, or very often kicked, bitten, hit with a fist, or hit with something hard? or
   - Ever repeatedly hit over at least a few minutes or threatened with a gun or knife?

   If yes, enter 1 _____

8. Did you live with anyone who was a problem drinker or alcoholic, or who used street drugs?

   If yes, enter 1 _____

9. Was a household member depressed or mentally ill, or did a household member attempt suicide?

   If yes, enter 1 _____

10. Did a household member go to prison?

   If yes, enter 1 _____

Now add up your "Yes" answers: _____
This is your ACE Score

Add up the points for a Score of 0 to 10. The higher the score, the greater the exposure, and therefore the greater the risk of negative consequences. Read more at www.acestudy.org.

Note to Service Providers: One of the biggest obstacles that stood in my path from receiving the help and services I needed was recognizing that I had experienced multiple traumas (referred to as compounded trauma) and that it was affecting every part my life. Finding one's ACE score helps victims recognize their own past traumas and that trauma on top of trauma affects them in significantly debilitating ways. For instance, if you work with trafficking victims, it is very important to remember that trafficking is only one aspect of how the person before you came to be in their current state of mind. It's highly likely that they have been exposed to multiple instances of trauma before receiving services. Getting to the roots, their background, is extremely beneficial in understanding how they got to be in the chair (or behind the bars) across from you. Whatever population you are working with, I recommend starting with or including in some part of your assessment process, the ACE questionnaire. When you do, you become a trauma-informed provider. Integrating it into your assessment process will help your volunteers and staff better understand how to help, but also provide an eye-opening experience for the test-taker who now has an opportunity to begin releasing shame, and to realize their present situation has more to do with something that happened to them than a personal career goal of being trafficked.

Resilience

Recognizing resiliency is just as important as understanding a person's background. Grief and depression are common effects of learning for the first time that present behaviors and hurts are inexplicably tied to past childhood trauma. A messed up childhood shoved to a dark corner of the mind, sealed with duct tape never to be opened again, now brought out of its cave. For some it brings relief; for others, depression.

Although we weren't designed with a dedicated drawer in our brains in which to put trauma away, we have protective factors that make us resilient, thereby offsetting some of the trauma. In a sense, without external interventions, trauma creates an invisible cast around the trauma brain that thickens with each additional bad experience. Thankfully our brains can heal. They are resilient. Learning to utilize resiliency aids the healing process and provides relief. More about using protective factors and resiliency to offset adverse childhood experiences is addressed in a subsequent chapter.

I remember when I first told my story. It didn't include my childhood abuse—events that happened without my consent and beyond my control. It only included the part about being trafficked—an event that I thought was in my control. At that time, that was all I knew and all that I recognized, but it was the only type of victimization for which I had a name. I thought trafficking was the whole story. As the months passed and I learned more about trauma and abuse, each piece of my past trauma filled in another blank until before me was the whole picture.

Other Types of Trauma

Trauma and toxic stress comes in many forms (trauma and toxic stress are often used interchangeably). Even though we associate them with abuse, other forms of trauma unrelated to abuse, like the loss of a child or close loved one or losing your home in a fire, are serious forms of trauma as well.

Sexual Abuse

Sexual abuse is a trauma experience. We tend to think of it as fondling or inappropriate touching (something that has different meanings to different people), but sexual abuse comes in many forms, including rape (any type of forced or non-consensual penetration).

What many don't know about sexual abuse is that it doesn't even have to involve touching to be considered sexual abuse. Any type of sexual behavior that an adult engages in with a child is sexual abuse. Viewing pornography, rubbing the inside of one's thigh in front of children, kissing inappropriately without permission, asking a child to expose themselves are considered sexual abuse. Sadly, these are but a few forms of it.

On another level, when a child three years or more that engages in sexual behavior it is considered sexual abuse. While two children who are the same age act out together, and it may not by law be considered sexual abuse, there are still negative effects on the children's brain that mimic sexual abuse.[5] It is important to note that what we pass off as *curiosity* or *experimentation* when children *act out* sexual behaviors, we may be missing important warning signals that sexual abuse may have occurred and should be carefully and thoughtfully explored. Ignoring the behavior or assigning it as kids being kids is dangerous. When we do, we miss an opportunity to discover the roots, the where and how the behavior came about. Was there exposure to pornography? Did something happen at a sleepover? We also miss the opportunity to break the chain. If we become aware of a child showing another child a specific sexual act or engaging in one, we have the opportunity to get to the source and intervene in a thoughtful way. This breaks the cycle of abuse from continuing.

Talking to kids about inappropriate touching and sexual abuse needs to be done thoughtfully and carefully. Done incorrectly, kids may clam up and blame themselves, thereby adding years of unnecessary shame and trauma-based behaviors. Help is available on handling suspected sexual abuse in children. Please check the Resource section.

As much as we don't like to admit that innocent children are exposed to the horrors of sexual abuse, it happens every day in homes in the poorest to the richest neighborhoods. With technological advance comes increased exposure to pornography by children. The effects are long-lasting and now we know that it has the same effect as sexual abuse on children. Children exposed by another person to pornography, either accidentally or intentionally, are likely to start acting out sexually, developing an appetite to see more and actually seeking other pornographic images. Addiction to pornography isn't just an *adult* problem. Children can become addicted as well, and at a very young age.

I once worked with an 11-year-old girl who was addicted to pornography. She was referred to me because she was caught making sexual videos of herself and posting them online. Where did it start? She reported that she'd seen an ad for pornography while surfing the Internet, clicked on it, and then hopped from one porn site to the next. It didn't take long before she took the leap from *viewing* pornography to *making* pornography. Just three months was all it took. How could this have been prevented? Her online activity should have been restricted until she was older, or at the very least it should have been monitored by her parents along with software designed to block porn sites. These seem like easy solutions, but we cannot rely on restrictions.

We have to have conversations about sex and body safety when children are young. If they don't learn about if from us they will learn about it from someone with intentions opposite our own.

In another case, a man with a little boy bemoaned the end of his marriage. His wife grew tired of her husband's controlling behaviors, incessant demands for sex and insatiable hunger for pornography. On the surface it was easy to dislike him and judge him, but when his childhood trauma history was revealed, his counselor was shocked to discover that his mother used porn magazines to keep him occupied while she was busy trying to keep up with her drug habit.

Sexual abuse of children is a sad reality that imposes a life sentence on its victims.

Physical Abuse

Just as sexual abuse comes in many forms, so does physical abuse. Is it only hitting and leaving bruises or scratches that qualified abuse as physical? No. Physical abuse takes many shapes. While we think of it in the most obvious ways, it can range from destroying property in front of another person, threats of physical harm to another person, blocking another person from leaving or using the phone, or even raising a fist at someone. This may be new information for some. While classified as intimidation, it is also considered physical abuse because of the fear of harm to your body through these tactics. Some other types of physical abuse are:

- Biting
- Pinching
- Punching
- Slapping

- Pulling hair
- Burning
- Shoving
- Restraining[6]

It is never okay to inflict physical abuse on anyone.

Mental and Emotional Abuse

Mental abuse and emotional abuse are easier to keep hidden both by an abuser and by the victim. In the past, accusations of mental and emotional abuse were unheard of. In the rare event that abuse was discussed, it usually focused on the physical type. Now, mental and emotional abuse are being recognized as a viable form of abuse. Because of the inherent difficulty proving mental or emotional abuse, they are the hardest abuses to prove legally. In the absence of visible marks or a bloody lip, it remains a hidden abuse. Victims are slow to recognize it because of long-held societal beliefs that mental and emotional abuse don't exist. And they place blame on themselves. This type of abuse has an insidious nature as it burrows undetected, deep into its victim's core.

Do you know what mental or emotional abuse is? This type of abuse can come in the form of name-calling at one of the spectrum to the more insidious and stealth form called gaslighting, a term not widely known outside the mental health community but extremely common in relationships. So, what does it mean? It's a form of abuse that causes its victims to question their own feelings, instincts, sanity or perception of reality.[7] Here's an example: Some abusers control to the point of not allowing their partner to leave the house. When the victim brings up the behavior at a later point, the abuser says something like, "That never happened, you are just overly emotional and sensitive," or, "You are over reacting; that's not the way it happened. You're losing it." Over time, the victim begins doubting their sanity.

Mental and emotional abuse examples could fill the pages of a book. Too many to count, they are just as damaging as any other type of abuse. Our childhood rhyme, "sticks and stones may break my bones, but words will never hurt me" couldn't be further from the truth. Words can stay with your forever. No marks on the skin, but if we had magic x-ray glasses, scars on the inside would be revealed. They have long-lasting repercussions in the form of trauma, and they sometimes pass from one generation to the next. Some other examples of mental or emotional abuse are:

- Blaming you for their actions
- Calling you names of any kind, including "slut shaming"
- Threatening you that they will leave
- Making fun of you
- Make you feel less than them
- Using your family or children against you
- Stalking
- Isolating you from friends and family
- Neglect

Another form of abuse is another of the less noticeable types. The National Child Abuse and Neglect Data System[8] defines neglect as "a type of maltreatment that refers to the failure by the caregiver to provide needed, age-appropriate care although financially able to do so or offered financial or other means to do so".[9] Some examples of neglect are:

- Withholding food
- Ignoring a child's needs
- Being left alone for hours
- Children taking on adult roles by caring for themselves or siblings
- Abandonment
- Missing school for unjustified reasons like sleeping in or "not feeling like it"
- Not bathing, showering, or getting basic needs met by caregivers

Spiritual Abuse

Spirituality is a source of inspiration and hope for many, but it can also be used against an individual and turn into abuse. Big news stories about cults led by cult leaders like Jim Jones or Warren Jeffs populate our minds with the idea that spiritual abuse equates to cults that are far removed from us. Unfortunately, this prevents us from identifying it in our communities right under our noses. It can be devastating and used as form of control. Threatening your partner or a child with threats of hell if they don't clean the house or if they behave in a certain way can be a form of abuse. And, although seemingly unrelated to trauma, subscribing to a particular religious organization's beliefs when it uses those beliefs to harm you can also be considered abuse. At its core, spiritual abuse distorts spiritual well-being. The following are some examples of spiritual abuse:

- When religion or beliefs are used to force compliance with something against one's personal beliefs or values
- Using beliefs to shame instead of empower or inspire
- Using religion or beliefs for personal gain and manipulation

Community Trauma

There are other forms of trauma, racism and homophobia, that don't only happen one-on-one. Being prevented from the freedom to be who you are can having a devastating effect and can be difficult to overcome, especially when accompanied by repeated negative statements based on skin color, sexuality or disability.

As difficult as it is to navigate the world as a cognitively or emotionally well person, it's even harder for children with disabilities who have a higher rate of physical and sexual abuse than children without disabilities. One study reported 30 percent of trafficking cases in two Florida cities involved girls with intellectual disabilities."[10]

Unfortunately, the rates of community violence are increasing and minority children—whether minority in ethnicity, gender association, disability, or otherwise—are at a higher risk for trauma.

Common Themes

One day I was on my way to a conference with several of my friends who were at various stages of dealing with their childhood traumas and ongoing abuse. We were sharing about our unique abuses, how we reacted to them at the time and how they impacted our lives. We had all experienced very different types of abuse and none of our stories of things we endured, as children were even close to being similar. I said, "I wet the bed until I was fifteen." and my friend next to me said, "Wait, I wet the bed until I was eleven." Then, one after the next, every person in the van revealed that they too had wet the bed. We burst out in giggles and gave big high fives to each other. I can only imagine what an outsider overhearing this conversation might have thought. While it may have looked extremely awkward and strange from the outside, it was a moment of connection for us. Being able to connect with one another's vulnerabilities and recognize that even though we had all experienced very different forms of trauma that continued to affect us on a level we could all understand, it helped us all to realize that we were not alone.

Note to Survivors of Abuse: I would hope for nothing more in your life than for you to see the beauty within yourself, and that there is absolutely nothing wrong or broken about you. You deserve the world and you are worthy of a life of freedom and passion, and for your every dream to come true. If you are struggling with things in your current situation, it is a completely normal reaction to an abnormal situation. Abuse is wrong. You are not wrong. You are not alone.

There is a common theme between all the stories I hear and my own experiences. I want to be very careful not to generalize exploitation or trafficking, because it happens in many ways, but there is no denying that most stories start out with something along the lines of, "I was raped/molested at a young age, things went downhill, I was in and out of foster case or lacked stability, and wound up with a pimp." I think this is where individuals can pull away from the issues and feel like it doesn't or hasn't affected them, that this affects kids from other neighborhoods, states, or countries. People from *good communities* sometimes want to do something, but do not recognize that all of this starts at home and in our communities.

Note to Teachers: It is important to note that while we can talk about 101 ways that children may exhibit signs of abuse, there are children who may fall through the cracks because they do not show typical signs of abuse. Sometimes children who have straight A's and are involved in lots of activities are there to escape from home and get their minds off of whatever they are going through.

I cannot tell you how many times I have heard from young girls who cut or self-harm that they were labeled as *looking for attention*. Well, of course they are. They are desperately hurting. Instead of labeling, blaming and casting aside, it should prompt us to withhold judgment, exercise compassion and empathy, and provide a path to healing. Just because they look good from the outside—great parents and/or affluence, we should *never* make assumptions about what goes on behind closed doors, and we can never assume that this is just another kid being a kid. We need to inquire further. Could she possibly have been molested at home, a friend's home, or another family member's home? Has he witnessed domestic violence? Has she lost a parent? Do his parents fight in front of him?

It is easy and natural for us to looks at bad behavior as the result of traumatic experiences when those experiences are obvious, but it's also easy and natural to ignore trauma when the acting out behaviors aren't easily observed or confirmed. What if every child who had experienced trauma walked around with a bubble above their heads that listed the things they had gone through? Would you see them differently? Would you have more compassion for the homeless individual with a sign that wasn't asking for food but instead listed all of the traumas that they had experienced throughout their life?

Taking a *trauma first* approach is to treat each client, student, child, or friend as though there is a root cause as to why he or she is acting out, acting reserved, or exhibiting perfectionism. There is always more than meets the eye, and we need to be looking deeper into others to truly help each person. The best way to bring these things to light is to talk about them; we have to start the conversations to start the process of healing.

CHAPTER 3

Groomed on Mulberry Street

For a brief time my mother and I lived in a nice, two-story ranch home with a pool, barn and huge backyard on Mulberry Street. This period seemed to hold the promise of being a stable moment where things appeared to be getting better, and allowed me to almost feel okay with thinking positive thoughts about my life and myself. I was even beginning to feel like an average nine-year-old for that matter. The neighborhood was full of other children to play with, and I could finally suspend the need to feel like an adult all the time. Plus, I remember the home specifically feeling more like a mansion to my adolescent eyes—and a world far away from sharing a cramped two bedroom apartment with eight or nine constantly bickering people, not to mention the cockroaches.

The house on Mulberry Street belonged to my uncle, who lived there with his new wife and her children. My step-aunt had a daughter my same age, and she and I shared a room together. We really connected, which made both of us very happy. This also was the first time in my life I can remember having this kind of relationship with someone else, who in turn felt the same about me. I think our mutual feelings were probably the result of each of us experiencing so much in our nine short years of life. She was one of a very few people who gave me any sincere attention.

One day we were sitting on the floor talking with each other, and to this day I don't even remember how the conversation started, but she told me that when she was little, someone in her family *touched* her. Being able to relate I immediately and excitedly replied, "I had sex with my cousin!"

She looked back at me for a moment before saying, "Did you tell your mom?"

"No," I replied. "After my uncle caught us, he told me that if I promised not to do it again, he wouldn't tell my mom because she would have been really upset with me for doing it." My step cousin then told me she didn't think my uncle was correct, because when she told her mom what happened to her, her mom took care of it and then told her it was wrong for someone to touch her like that. She suggested that because my cousin was much older than me he should have known better.

Although I know there was a part of me that understood she was right, I was scared to be honest with my mother about what happened almost three years ago. My parent's divorce took a tremendous amount out of my mother, and the constant bouncing around between living situations afterward had not helped either. After she left my younger brother's dad, things with her only seemed to get worse. She was working an overnight shift that day, so even if I would have mustered the courage to talk with her, I couldn't at that moment.

My cousin was more upset by our discussion than I knew,

and it turns out she didn't wait for me to tell my mom anyway. She confessed our conversation to my step-aunt, and before I knew it a note appeared on my mother's bedroom door saying, "Savannah needs to talk to you." Despite my fear, and also because I had little choice otherwise at that point, after she came home that day I told my mom what happened to me those several years ago. Her reaction was nothing short of unbridled hysteria. She immediately ran to the phone and between bouts of screaming, hyperventilating, and crying she managed to call the police. Although the words coming out of her mouth were barely intelligible, the police understood enough to know why she was so upset.

Within the hour, two officers came to the house and picked us up. I was so afraid for so many reasons, but mainly I think it was because I was too young to fully understand exactly what was taking place and what might happen. In my young mind, because the incident had taken place several years beforehand, I still did not understand how bad it actually was. Beyond this, I was becoming very fearful that if it was so bad, then it was also my fault for participating in it. Before I could even begin to get my bearings, I found myself sitting in a tiny cement room with a video camera pointed straight at me as two male officers peppered me with one question after another.

My mom was on the other side of the glass crying, which I could easily hear. I felt very self-conscious as I was asked to show the officers, through the use of demonstrating on a stuffed animal, what my teenage cousin had done to my body. After all of the fear, drama and trauma this incident caused me, the official police report noted a number of discrepancies in my account. Because of this, nothing ever came of the matter—and the report, like so many others before and since, was dismissed.

Grooming and Human Trafficking

The account you're about to read will serve as the platform in our discussion about child abuse, as well as its relationship to human trafficking and other forms of social injustice. Grooming is a term used to describe the process in which a pimp/trafficker/abuser manipulates a victim through the employment of coercive physical, mental, or emotional tactics. It's used to prepare the victim to be trafficked, which ensures the likelihood that the victim will submit to the will and intentions of the perpetrator while being less apt to flee or resist.

This is why this chapter is titled "Groomed on Mulberry Street." My experience is that for many, including myself, the grooming process starts well before the initial interaction with a pimp, trafficker or abuser. Rather, it usually begins with that first instance of trauma, followed by either an absence of intervention, even a harmful intervention, which ushers in a snowball effect of reoccurring, compounded trauma. This unfortunate series of events effectively influences the victim into thinking such behavior is normal, natural, deserved or imminent. It is this internal alteration of conscious interaction and functioning that allows a victim to become a candidate for human trafficking.

The phrase *human trafficking* is by definition incredibly non-specific. Without common language between professionals and clinicians to standardize various components, interventions, and ideologies, it is also confusingly generalized at times. Even with the significant rise in anti-trafficking efforts, there remains incredibly varied ideas about how to deal with both victims and their experiences in their entirety. It is my experience that not just one individual or single organization can or will ever address all of the needs inherent in the discussion. A discussion, might I add, that is long overdue for society to have—despite how uncomfortable it might make some people. It is this kind of taboo treatment of such a longstanding and ongoing issues that has allowed it to persist to the present day.

Therefore, the only way to effectively combat the human trafficking epidemic facing us is through collaboration, unique approaches, and communication between clients, clinicians, and other industry professionals in order to elicit the most significant and sweeping changes. My passion and proficiency for this subject lies in a few different areas, but mostly focuses on trauma-informed approaches and prevention. Addressing, understanding, talking about, and de-stigmatizing conversations around trauma and abuse is the most effective approach to putting the person before any labels, diagnoses, or stigmas that much more than they help.

Prevention Conversations

When I train others and perform speaking engagements, I use my personal experiences as a source of public education. I begin each talk by talking about my parent's attempts to teach me about sexual abuse before I ever experienced it. I have found, based on conversations with hundreds of parents, that this information mimics the conversations many parents have with their children. They typically lack important contextual information that would otherwise make those conversations more effective. In this context, the following statements were the ones my mother and father made to me about sexual abuse and stranger danger when I was a child. These conversation were not wrong, but we do need to go deeper.

As mentioned earlier, I happened to have one of those fathers who was invested in teaching me about safety and self-defense. Both my mother and father were adamant about preventing me from experiencing any form of abuse. They made a good effort to educate me. What I learned from them were good starting points for any parent-child conversation on this topic. However, it would have been better to bring them up multiple times. They told me:

- If someone ever touches your private parts, tell mommy or daddy right away. If we aren't around, tell someone you trust. Never be afraid to tell, because you are not in trouble or at fault

- No one except mommy or daddy are allowed to touch you on your private parts when we give you a bath, or if the doctor is checking you but only with mommy or daddy in the room

- If someone tries to kidnap you, kick and scream "you are not my mommy, you are not my daddy"

- You can also scream "fire" if no one listens, because people will listen and respond when they hear that word

A good starting point, yes. When I was growing up, parents could not Google "ways to talk to your kids about body safety." Yet, this small list of conversation starters are no different from those that many reputable authorities online and elsewhere recommend that parents have with their children today. When talking with friends, family and those I interact with through my various training and speaking engagements, this rings accurate across the board. These conversations are a great tool to begin teaching children about body safety. However, and as you have read thus far, due to the various types of trauma and abuse I experienced, or the effective grooming if you will, such conversations and self-defense tactics were not enough to help me learn to protect myself.

It must be said that sometimes such conversations never take place between parents and their children, possibly due to stigma, shame or embarrassment. Some adults deny the possibility that trauma and abuse can befall their children, or are uncertain about when the right age or time to have these conversations is, so they end up never having them at all. Other parents feel that by having these conversations, they will actually implant ideas in their child's mind about sex, or that these conversations will give children the impetus to act out sexually.

Finally it must be said, and to no great surprise I am sure, that in our society we don't want to talk children about sex or private parts because it is generally considered taboo. We want them to be and stay little children, to play safely and securely while remaining ignorant of anything other than that reality for as long as possible. After all, we have a lot of important things on our minds as parents as it is. Are they getting a good education? Are they eating the right kind of food? Are we able to juggle their extracurricular activities and homework?

I have four children, plus I go to school and work, so there is no lack of eventfulness in our lives. I understand firsthand both the demands and the go-go-go pattern of living that parents, myself included, get caught up in. I also know I am not with my children every minute of every day and because of this reality, these conversations may be the most important part of parenting. The effort I put into their futures every day can easily be undone by an incident of trauma or abuse that can lead them down a road of low self-worth and negative self-image. This state of mind invariably leads many people to engage in unhealthy relationships with self and others, not to mention addiction and even death.

Yes, such internal struggles can definitely be rectified and overcome, but hopefully by having these uncomfortable yet important conversations with our children we will prevent abuse by stopping it from happening in the first place. Prevention must begin with changing the way we talk to our children or the ones close to us.

How should parents discuss body safety? How should parents respond and get children the help they need and deserve when and if the unthinkable ever happens?

Good and Bad Reactions

A dear friend of mine took steps to teach her children about body safety, just as my parents did with me. When her girls reached age five she even stopped washing their body parts, instead encouraging them to wash themselves while letting them know how important their bodies are—so much so that not even mommy and daddy are not allowed to touch them in these situations. Yet, several years later, she was blindsided and devastated upon learning that her ex-husband had sexually assaulted their two daughters. Sadly, this is not unusual. According to dosomething.org, family members are involved in 68% of all reported sexual abuse cases[1]. Today, because of our experiences, both of us talk with our kids much more proactively and supportively about abuse and body safety. Our conversations are ongoing and natural, and we use everyday opportunities to talk about safety and boundaries. We don't shield are kids from experiencing the world we give them the tools to navigate it with emotional intelligence. For example we don't just talk about body safety we teach it, by never forcing them to hug or kiss someone they don't want to. This is one example and I will talk about more solutions later in the book.

It is important to understand why, despite a parent's best intentions and periodic discussions with children about body safety, children still keep this terrible secret. I have spoken with many people who have recovered from trauma to pick their brains about the factors that played into their decisions to stay silent. The reasons are many.

I failed to disclose my abuse to my parents, even though my parents taught me much more about body safety than my friend's parents. There are several factors that played into my decision to stay silent, and to eventually be honest.

Why I DID Disclose My Abuse

My step-cousin disclosed her abuse to me first. This was a powerful experience, as it gave me the courage to talk about what had happened to me even though at that time I didn't fully understand what took place. Today when I speak and share my experiences with others, whether professionals or high school students, many teens and adults disclose abuse to me for the same reason. From physically violent relationships and rape to everything in between, they tell me that my courage inspires them to be honest, too.

It is not necessarily the *type* of trauma that connects people, but simply acknowledging that the other person has experienced something similar. I believe mutual honesty and respect is one of the most effective ways to empower others to find their own voice. No survivor should ever feel pressured to tell the stories they've buried, but those who can will undoubtedly have a profound impact on others.

Sometimes an intimate interpersonal discussion can help someone open up about their own abuses and traumas much more so than in a crowded room, including meeting a caring stranger in a place you would never expect like on an airplane or in the aisle of a grocery store aisle. My children are always asking me, "Can we just get the milk or do you have to make friends with everyone you meet?" In one instance, I was on a plane flying home from a sex trafficking conference. Seated next to a man in his forties, conversation flowed after the initial awkward introduction when people ask what each other does for a living. After listening quietly, he stopped me and disclosed that he too had experienced sexual abuse. In his case, a babysitter molested him. It was the first time in his life he had told anyone. Merely talking briefly about my sexual abuse history helped bring down his walls and open the door, even just a little. It was a powerful moment for both of us, one that's repeated everywhere I go.

From my perspective, that house on Mulberry Street was a stable place. I had healthy interactions and went to school with people I got along with. Those relationships represented the first time in a long time I had not been ostracized by my peers. There was plenty of food, stable shelter, as well as other children for me to play with and feel normal around. Overall I felt safe, secure, and relaxed enough to disclose.

This is a very important piece of the equation for any victim of abuse and trauma. If someone is stuck in survival mode, their brain functions in a constant state of hyper-arousal. They are often only thinking moment-to-moment, and surviving from one day to the next. Having a sense of stability, safety and security helps them begin to process and make connections with what is going on in and around them. This goes for adults and children alike and it's another reason people tend to disclose when they hear other peoples' experiences—it gives them a sense of safety and similarity with that person, and one in which they don't fear judgment or repercussions from disclosing.

Why I Did NOT Disclose

Despite all of the informative conversations my parents had with me about body safety, I still didn't disclose the incident with my cousin until years after the fact. This is important because this reaction was the catalyst for many of the other abusive and traumatic experiences I would have going forward.

Even though my uncle came into the room shortly after the abuse happened, and he indeed got the feeling something inappropriate had just taken place, he responded with punishment instead of understanding. He grabbed us by the hair and made us face the wall. Punishment. He probably thought he was doing the right thing by making us promise to never do it again or he'd tell our mothers.

His response, aside from being totally inappropriate, was incredibly damaging for several reasons:

- It placed blame on me—I thought it was my fault
- It taught me that sexual abuse was something that was to remain a secret, hidden from my parents
- It provided no follow-up to prevent future abuses or psychological issues from occurring.

Because my abuser referred to the act he committed as sex,

instead of understanding it as something performed against my will—rape—I thought I was just *having sex*. Because of this, I began to internalize and associate sex with an act forced upon me, instead of understanding it as rape and the associated trauma, abuse and hurt.

At the same time, my parents were going through their divorce. My home life and interpersonal relationships were unstable, and my daily routine was chaotic. This alone might not be considered devastating to a child in some situations, especially with positive co-parenting, but in my case, my mom's life was instable. She moved to another state where she relied on family members to get her through.

The instability of my home life combined with the act perpetrated against me, reinforced my vulnerability. Disclosure became synonymous with fear, shame and a further disruption of my already traumatic family and life situations.

What Went Right When I Disclosed

First and foremost, my mom believed me even when other family members denied it and accused me of being a liar.

To this day, I appreciate my mother more than words can say for calling the police to report the rape even though the incident took place three years prior and the subsequent interrogation was less than pleasant. I realize that some people may condone her actions as standard operating procedure in the unwritten book of parenting. Unfortunately, her reaction is not nearly as common as one might assume. One of the reasons I do not like using a plethora of statistics regarding sexual abuse is because ultimately all of the numbers we have are just the tip of a much larger and more troublesome iceberg. Despite the fact that my mom was less likely to positively intervene because she herself had experienced unreported sexual abuse and trauma throughout her life, she did things right. She believed me, she reported it, she protected me from others who did not believe me, and she got me enrolled in counseling.

Even though I didn't know it then, I certainly know now that my cousin who disclosed to me first actually responded beautifully to my revelation in many ways. She told me that what happened to me was wrong and she encouraged me to tell someone. She let me know that an adult should handle a situation like this and even made sure one would whether I was ready to disclose or not. Due to the intervention her mother provided for her, and all of the conversations she had with adults in her life, she felt empowered enough to protect and support me that day on the floor of her bedroom.

She at young age advocated for me, that is something that is very different for my own children today, they don't only advocate for them selves but for others.

What Happened That was Harmful

Some of my family did not believe me, and even insulted and ostracized me. It is not uncommon for families to react this way when an abuse victim finally reveals the truth. It's so damaging.

When families or others don't believe a child, they don't realize they are consciously protecting the abuser. It must be stated here that it is extremely rare for a child to make up an account of abuse, although it does happen. It's imperative that every accusation is taken seriously and investigated to determine whether it is true or false. There are cases of false accusations, particularly in high-conflict divorce cases, but even then it is not the child making the false accusation. The percentage of false accusations are actually quite low and often those are victims who recant due to shame and stress or a child who has reported that they were assaulted but do not name the actual abuser because of fear.

More of the harmful fallout:

- It caused conflict that I felt responsible for
- No intervention took place to contradict the feeling of blame and shame
- Organizations like Child Help and other family advocacy centers were either not in existence or not widely used. I was taken to a police station and had to show a male officer exactly had happened to me three years prior, by another male. Honestly that was more stressful and traumatizing for me than anything else
- There were no repercussions for my abuser
- The choice to not move forward with an investigation was not mine
- The counselor that I saw did not address my trauma. In fact, we only talked about my feelings about my abuse and my anger toward my abuser. Interestingly, at that point I did not have anger toward my abuser because I still did not fully understand what had happened, so I ended up saying what I thought everyone wanted to hear instead
- At that time I never received any education about what abuse looked like, or what the effects of abuse are, in either an age appropriate way or otherwise
- There was never a point that I felt safe and comfortable enough to, or was given the knowledge of how to, identify

abuse. This influenced my non-disclosure of the co-occurring sexual abuse that started at age seven by another family member, and that continued well into my teens. No one ever asked, and so no one knew the other abuses were being committed

- We had to move again, so my home life was very unstable and I was switching schools a lot. This caused a lack of peer-to-peer relationships, family support, as well as a safe and comfortable atmosphere with which to have open discussions about the abuses

- My parents did not receive the education they needed in order to support me at the necessary level

Every person's family dynamics are different. The way people respond or do not response to abuse and trauma is also different. I have spoken a lot here about sexual abuse as trauma, mostly because childhood sexual abuse and human trafficking are connected in this regard. However, other forms of trauma including physical abuse, neglect, institutional oppression, community violence and domestic violence also come into play when we talk about the trafficking demographic.

Note to Educators: Disclosure of abuse is a very frightening thing for a child to do in a school setting. It takes hours to make a report of child abuse. As teachers, you already have a million mandates, constant budget cuts, and other everything else to keep up with. Add to it, each district seems to have different policies on handling abuse allegations. Some districts only allow principals to file reports, and some states have moved to online reporting. Unfortunately, the issue begins to focus on the reporting process instead of the disclosure and the child. As an educator, your focus should not just be on responding to disclosures, but also about understanding that the children in your classroom face adversities that change the way they learn, to the point of impacting their overall ability to learn. Most importantly, no child should ever have to disclose abuse in order to receive empathy in the classroom. I had many "safe" teachers that have greatly impacted my life and I never disclosed to them, what I remember is them listening and caring for me no matter how I acted.

Everyone has their own experience and it won't be exactly like mine, nor do we all react and respond the same way. Our development and experiences determine our resilience. Each person's story is their own.

We must learn what to do when abuse is disclosed by a child, or even when we suspect it. We must be prepared with policies that provide the structure needed to support and protect children and we must foster a safe environment for children to learn, grow, and heal. Childhood abuse does not need to ruin a child's life. With the appropriate intervention, love and support, healing can happen and life can be free of the anxieties and stress that come with untreated trauma.

The earlier we intervene, the more effective interventions will be. We can create positive outcomes.

Let's pause a moment to remember that not every child who experiences childhood trauma will become a victim of sex trafficking. However, trafficking, in addition to unhealthy relationships with self and others, is much more likely to occur when that trauma is compounded by improper or non-existent interventions.

Note to Service Providers: A child or and adult does not need to disclose abuse in order to receive beneficial psycho education. We don't need a disclosure from the person in front of us to begin making important human connections. I cannot tell you how many young girls and boys I meet who engage in cutting or who have even attempted suicide that have absolutely no conscious thought that these behaviors and actions may be reactions to trauma. This even applies to those currently receiving services from clinicians and professionals who do not utilize trauma informed care to help get to the root of why the behavior came into existence in the first place. No one has ever taken the time to explain the correlations between their actions and their trauma, so these young people are left helpless to understand and help themselves.

Many children do not have a support system at all, and in some cases their traffickers or abusers are their parents or close family members. The information presented here should be applicable whether you are a parent, a service provider working with a family or caregiver, an educator, or any other positive influence in a child or adult's life. As you have read here, even our best intentions and attempts at conversation do not stave off abuse and trauma 100 percent of the time. Despite our best efforts to this effect, children may not disclose for a number of reasons. So what can we do to intervene, or at least support them if they do not tell us something has occurred?

• Creating a safe, comfortable and trusting environment is key. Yes, there may be things going on in all of our lives at the time, but that does not mean we cannot work diligently to create safety wherever we are. I heard a beautiful story about a teacher who asked her kids before class began each day if they had eaten and brushed their teeth. She took time every morning to make sure each child's needs were met before starting the school day. By doing this, she created safety in the space she had to work with. We can all follow her example no matter our title, job, or role

- Learning about the signs and stages, as well as overall experiences accompanying abuse and trauma, even when someone has not experienced it

- Classic dark alley, trench coat style sexual abuse education is not enough. A large percentage of abusers are either family members or close friends. We have to move beyond stranger danger education and into a realm of self-awareness, trust and comfort

- At the end of the day we often have to rely on our instincts. Not everyone will have the awareness or the strength to tell you they have been wrongfully treated, but if we are aware of the warning signs then we can use non-verbal cues to help support, if not directly intervene at that point

CHAPTER 4

How We All Can Intervene

Despite all our best efforts, some people choose not to disclose their abuses and traumas. There are many different signs and symptoms of abuse that we can educate ourselves to recognize, and it is of the utmost importance that we do just this. In the Introduction, we discussed how an abuser or trafficker spots vulnerabilities in potential victims and then uses them to exploit that person for his or her own gain. We need to be equally aware of these vulnerabilities by arming ourselves with the same knowledge the predators have in order to intervene with the hope of providing empowerment instead of exploitation.

Before we dive into the different signs and symptoms of trauma, it is important to note that a child who exhibits some of these signs doesn't automatically indicate abuse or trauma. The last thing we want is for adults to convince themselves that children have been abused every time a possible red flag is spotted. Just because a young child has trouble potty training does not necessarily indicate abuse, but if a teenage child is wetting the bed or having accidents in their clothing, that is definitely cause for concern and further investigation. Being aware of the existence of these types of symptoms helps construct a platform where deeper conversations can be conducted in a comfortable, safe, non-threatening, and non-accusatory manner and environment.

Red Flags

Bed-wetting can be one of the signs that a child has experienced trauma. There are several reasons why people of all ages wet their beds, and there also exists a diverse array of literature one can procure from doctors as well as many reputable online authorities regarding helping those who struggle with bed-wetting.

It must be stated here though that many of these pieces of literature fail to mention trauma as a possible root cause of bed-wetting. My pediatrician's office has a wall poster stating that one in four children wets the bed, and then goes on to list reasons why this behavior might be occurring. It lists biological factors, developmental delays, and so on and so forth. What is not listed anywhere on the poster is trauma, even though research has found a direct correlation between the two. I suppose then that it's not a coincidence that I and many of my friends who experienced trauma and abuse experienced involuntary bed-wetting as a pre-teen or teen.

Another red flag commonly seen in trauma victims is fear of the dark. One of my daughters is terrified of the dark. She is so afraid of the dark that she's afraid to visit the bathroom on her own at night because she is scared to be alone anywhere— even if we are in the living room and she is in the kitchen. Her fear arises from a pretty severe sensory integration problem that causes her extreme anxiety though, and is not the result of abuse or trauma initiating such behavior.

Compulsive lying is also a red flag, as well as constantly creating ailments or illnesses. My other daughter's first reaction to any questioning is to lie the second we ask about anything. It is usually an instantaneous response though, and then a moment later she confesses the truth. She is also the child who will tell me that everything hurts whether or not she bangs her arm or leg against the wall. Our universal response is usually, "Okay, well don't do that and it won't hurt." But despite her flair for the dramatic, she is also not being abused or traumatized either.

Though the preceding behaviors are commonly cited as being red flags for abuse and trauma, I purposely used my girls as examples to demonstrate that when taken alone, these behaviors are not necessarily signs of abuse. Rather, they are normal adolescent reactions comprising the experience of growing up. Each one of my children is unique and therefore responds to life in his or her individualized and personalized ways. You can probably find a warning sign or potential red flag in every child, but it is important to take a contextual look at the whole human being in question before convincing yourself there exists a need for further action. This being said, if you have or encounter a child exhibiting a combination of these symptoms, or extreme yet unexplained cases of any one of them, then it becomes time to take a closer and more critical look at what might be causing the behaviors.

My Red Flags

I feel it important to discuss the signs I exhibited throughout my younger childhood years in order to provide you with an idea of what to look for when deciding whether or not to entertain abuse and trauma as a reason for behavior. After my initial incident at age six, and from the ages of seven to twelve years old, I was left incredibly vulnerable to further abusers. They were able to sense my vulnerabilities, which is why the lack of an initial intervention was so detrimental to me. The adolescent years are the most crucial for proactive, early intervention. This is why it is so very important for parents, caregivers and anyone who works around children to learn the signs and symptoms of abuse and trauma.

Again I will state that these examples were specific to me, and how I dealt with trauma and abuse. Other people may display and react differently than I did, but the following nevertheless remains an informed and insightful reference point.

The ways I changed after trauma:

- I started wetting the bed when I was about seven or eight years old. I was potty trained pretty early in life. After toddlerhood I did not have accidents at night until shortly after my abuses and traumas began. My father tried to intervene by reading literature and cutting off my drinks at a certain time in the evening, but none of this helped of course. By the age of ten or eleven, wetting the bed at night correlated with having a difficult day. If I felt rejected or got into a fight with my mom, I knew there was a higher chance of it happening, so I attempted to regulate my fluid intake and make sure I went to the bathroom right before bed. At that time I was not actively aware that my abuses were causing this behavior. Furthermore, my parents had no idea I was looking deeply enough into my own routine so as to warrant such measures. Based on the complexity and dysfunction of our relationship, I unfortunately had to act as my own caretaker more often than not back then

- I started to lie all of the time. I felt as though I had to exaggerate even the most minute details, and I often made up entire stories for no reason whatsoever

- I started becoming increasingly sexualized far beyond what is considered normal for any corresponding age. I made sexually oriented jokes regularly, and attempted to act older than I was in my mannerisms and behaviors

- I started becoming increasingly aggressive with my mother and father. I began saying things like "I hope you die," and my anger became extreme to the point of regular verbal and even physical altercations

- As my behaviors caused me to lose friends and isolate from my peers, I began attaching to adults instead of people my own age

- My academic behavior and performance changed drastically for the worse. I was constantly getting in trouble because I was not able to focus, constantly losing or neglecting my homework, and engaging in negative, attention-seeking behavior during class time

- I was terrified of the dark, and would spend many nights lying on the couch shaking in fear long after everyone else went to bed. I would watch cartoons to curb the fear until I could no longer keep my eyes open and literally just pass out.

A Note about Trauma-Informed Care: If my parents had known why I was behaving like this, they could have at least had the opportunity to successfully intervene. My trauma needed to be addressed, but for this matter and in the absence of that, simply leaving the light on at night when

I went to sleep would have helped to some degree. I have spoken with many parents that tell me their children are afraid of the dark, and even some who say their children confess to seeing things, but only at night. Of course, the heightened anxiety caused by their fear most likely causes them to see things that are really not there. These parents tell me that providing a nightlight still doesn't quell the child's fear. In these cases, it is okay to take extra steps like leaving the main light on to ensure the child feels safe. That is really what trauma-informed care is all about: Identifying existing barriers and then creating ways to work within ones current environment—in order to help the individual feel safe and secure. This is just one example but it adequately demonstrates the fact that the best and biggest difference we can make in the lives of those we care about is not assuming what works for us will work for them, too. Rather, in these situations we must employ our empathy and compassion to allow us to listen to and provide for the specific needs of the individual in question as they request it.

Just about every behavior I described is now considered a commonly accepted symptom of trauma. I would have been considered a textbook case, so to speak, even if at the time of my abuses no textbook existed with which to draw insight from.

Delving Beneath the Behavior

The ACE Study, mentioned in Chapter 2, documents an increased risk of intravenous drug use, suicide attempts, and self-deprecating behavior in people who have experienced trauma versus those who have not. It is not at all uncommon for an trauma survivor to venture down one or more of these paths if no intervention occurs. Of course, as time goes by and age increases, the likelihood of issues arising from unreconciled trauma only grow as well. This is why trauma-informed care is so promising and positive. Trauma-informed care looks beneath the surface at the root cause of what eventually becomes risky behaviors—instead of just judging or stigmatizing someone for the behavior itself.

Let's take a look at the following example that lends contextual insight into this reality. You have a family with two children and both children experience the same traumas within the home, yet both grow up with varying perspectives on the events and how they affect them. You may have one that shows several prominent red flag warning signs, while the other may go the complete opposite direction—perfect grades, never making a major life mistake, and doing their best to exhibit the belief that everything in life is totally okay. Instead of engaging in risky behavior like child A, child B strives for absolute perfection and only gets upset when they cannot achieve that standard.

I knew a set of twins who were both sexually abused. By the time one of them was in elementary school, she was already incredibly aggressive, bullied other students, and got suspended multiple times. Her identical twin sister was the complete opposite. She was shy and reserved, got along with everyone, had phenomenal grades, and was involved in several extracurricular activities. Each child responded to her trauma differently, yet one was supported and celebrated while the other continued to be punished for behaviors resulting from her traumas. No one knew of the abuses. Each twin was judged solely on her actions, instead of the intent or reasons behind them.

In no way, shape or form does this mean we shouldn't question children who get good grades. We should make it a point to get to know, understand and treat every child with dignity and empathy no matter his or her actions. Often, we do not know the full story even where our children are concerned—and this lack of knowledge, especially when combined with the hubris of supposition, can end up harming much more than helping.

Note to Educators: Trauma-informed care for children in school is not about becoming an abuse or trauma dictation machine. It is about making sure every child in the classroom has a supportive, comfortable, healthy and happy learning environment they can thrive and be themselves in.

Recognizing the Symptoms While Seeing to the Cause

Some red flags are more apparent and concerning than others and as we discussed earlier, looking for a combination of symptoms is key. I exhibited several symptoms, but they did not all manifest overnight or at the same time. Rather, I began exhibiting a couple at a time, and this subtle but apparent presence allowed the predators to tune into my vulnerabilities. First my parents divorced, then I was raped, and after which I started being periodically molested, which also coincided with constantly relocating from one living space and place to the next.

Each of these events compounded my trauma, which caused my risky behaviors to increase. This increase then further affected the way I responded to the traumas, causing my symptoms to become more severe and behaviors even more complicated. It was at this time my father and teachers unsuccessfully began attempting behavioral modification. My father would sit down with me and help with my homework, as well as check my backpack every night to make sure I didn't lose or hide anything. My teachers tried separating me from my peers so I could focus. Many people tried with the best of intentions to help me, but it never worked because they were too focused on the behaviors rather than the unheeded and treated situations and circumstances causing these behaviors to manifest in the first place.

Granted this portion of my story took place more than twenty years ago, and things have changed a bit in our society. We have behavioral therapy and interventions now that didn't exist when I was growing up. Because of this evolution in consciousness, my hope is that if I were in school today and acted the way I did then, someone might have inquired about, investigated the cause and helped me find support. There are several different procedures today that were not available to me then: Parents are more likely to be called in for a conference about their child's behavior, 504 and Individual Education Plans (IEP's) are sometimes instituted, and referrals for psychological evaluations are more commonly prescribed. Admittedly, not all of these options can help all children. However, even though these and other resources are available, the biggest issue and concern is that they all still primarily focus on the behavior being exhibited and not the root cause.

In no way am I saying interventions such as those mentioned above have no purpose. In fact, they can be of a great benefit to some children. One of my children has a speech delay and is considered to be on the autistic spectrum, mainly for sensory integration difficulties. She experiences immense social anxiety, has prominent Obsessive Compulsive tendencies, and while she was excelling in some facets of school, she struggled emotionally and socially. Her IEP's and the school's support system have been incredibly effective for her growth. That can best be measured in wonderful leaps and bounds.

However, we must bear in mind the fact that she has not experienced a trauma or abuse that caused her struggles to occur in the first place. Whether or not the intervention would have been as successful as it is if she had is something we will never know—but it is important to note that trauma was never even considered to be a root cause by any educator, clinician or professional involved in her intervention process. Trauma is usually the least inquired about and most overlooked cause of behavioral issue. This tendency to dismiss it must be remedied if we want to change it.

While my daughter's therapies have helped her immensely, these same types of interventions would not have been effective in my situation because the root cause of my behaviors was not being properly or even consciously addressed. It's true that I had several interventions during those chaotic years, I was still experiencing trauma during these times. Because of this I did not understand the abuse as an active cause of my behavior. Furthermore, my parents were not being educated to properly support me, and no industry professional was inquiring as to what I had been through that resulted in me acting out as I was.

Whether anyone has personally overseen the disclosure of a child who has experienced trauma, we know enough as a society to know without a shadow of a doubt that trauma is not as uncommon an occurrence as some would like to believe. Because of this prevalent reality, we owe it to our children to start incorporating trauma-informed approaches into our personal and professional environments. Only by doing so do we stand the chance of fundamentally and positively impacting a person's life, even if we are not aware of that person's specific experiences and potential struggles.

Recognition Must Precede Reconciliation

When you think about the children in and around your life, can you think of anyone who may be exhibiting signs of abuse? Remember, showing one sign is usually not a red flag, and it is not uncommon for every child to exhibit a unique combination of signs and symptoms during adolescence. However, being and remaining aware of abuse as a contributing factor to behavioral problems can greatly benefit our systems of care and sense of community alike. We do not have to have all of the answers in order to make a difference, but if we take steps to identify the signs of child abuse and other traumas, we can at least begin to usher in the all-important processes of identifying and intervening—which of course are both essential foundations of realizing and facilitating healing.

Life during traumas is most definitely not replete with rainbows and sunshine, and neither is recovery. Every person's situation, circumstances and overall experiences are their own and unique. Speaking about my experiences specifically, working through my abuses and traumas has been one of the most difficult, painful, and at times unsettling things I have ever done. However, I can also personally attest to a new life of happiness, freedom and hope. They truly exist if you persevere by continuing to unpack and reconcile the past traumas.

Even though my own journey has included tremendous amounts of suffering and pain, I remain grateful and thankful for all of my experiences. For only by overcoming those experiences have I become the person I am today. Granted, it has been a stepped and sometimes steep process to reach this point of awareness, acceptance and accomplishment in and of myself. My success lends directly into my sincere belief that every person has the ability to experience the same success, happiness and health I have—should they choose to undertake their own individualized journey of recovery that is supported by a system that facilitates healing.

CHAPTER 5

Signs and Prevention Efforts for Teens

Every time I tell people that I have a teenage daughter, reactions are always a mixture of generalized sympathy or support. Warnings of the precarious a journey I'm in for are shared with vehemence. The teenage years are treated with a sense of impending doom by parents and anyone else teenagers regularly interact with.

Misunderstandings and misrepresentations persist when we think about the teenage years. It's not much of a stretch to say that adults actually cause teenage angst to occur much more so than teenagers themselves. Whether it is through society, education or home, the belief the word *teenager* is synonymous with rebelliousness actually breeds exactly that which is feared. To combat this self-fulfilling manifestation, adults tend to go to one extreme or the other in order to manage their teenagers. Some become helicopter parents and others become absentee landlords.

Despite the best intentions of any parent in question, many teens still have little or no tangible, compassionate, or real-world guidance to help navigate this phase of life. The reasons are many, but for the purposes of our discussion we can relate this back to chapter 3 and the reasons why some parents do not discuss sex and body safety with their children. Parenting is a learning process, and they don't always get it right.

Sometimes parents are subconsciously guilty of ignoring that which they are uncomfortable addressing. They instead put their faith in society, including education, to discuss uncomfortable or unfamiliar topics with their children for them. The danger inherent in this reasoning is that more often than not, this avoidance results in the absence of values and ethics, not to mention critical decision-making skills being instilled into their children.

Some children will successfully make their own way despite a lack of parental guidance and compassion. Others, however, will end up traveling a much less positive path. And while some of those wandering down this darker path enter it during these years exclusively, others were already prepped and groomed to enter it based on traumatic incidents and experiences that happened before entering the teen years.

When combined with the stigma, isolation and physiological alterations that come with the teenage experience, symptoms that might have remained either dormant or minimized in younger years can rocket into prominence with little or no warning. These unfortunate kids end up labeled many different ways, and though many people will undoubtedly try to modify their behaviors, very few will be committed enough to take the time to understand why these behaviors exist in the first place.

When children make mistakes, the acceptable answer is usually behavioral modification. Along these lines tough love, isolation, and incarceration are used as threats toward teens that either can't or don't see the future that adults desire for them. In reality, these are kids who are able to do little more than survive until the next day. While people may think that behavioral modification, including threats will help a teenager in distress, in most cases it only pushes them further away. It also serves to mask and suppress the root causes of their distress even more than they were before.

Developmentally, adolescents are prone to taking more risks, experience diminished impulse control, and, of course, not enjoying being surrounded by judgmental adults most of the time. Certainly the teenage years are difficult for any young adult, but for those who have experienced trauma in some way, the path is exponentially more daunting and dangerous. For teens that do not receive empathetic and compassionate interventions and support, these years can be fatal.

That is why it is up to all adults to be diligent and vigilant. We must not only be watchful, we need to set the proper examples and influence them in a positive way. By taking a trauma-informed approach to interactions with teenagers, adults can become positive and proactive agents for guidance and change in the lives of teens who otherwise may only bounce back and forth between one of the two main extremes many adults employ with interpersonal interaction and intervention.

Teenage Red Flag Warnings

By the time I entered my preteen years, I started grasping at social straws by desperately trying to connect with anyone in any group. When I was 12, my need for friendships and relationships to save me from looking at myself became very intense. No matter how I presented myself on the outside, I was lonely and miserable on the inside. Because of this self-loathing, entering relationships resulted in latching on too tightly, which usually just pushed people away. Or this is how it worked in my interactions with healthy people at least. The harder it became for me to fit in anywhere, the deeper I got into self-destructive behaviors like drug use, self-harm and isolating myself from anyone who cared. All my hope for reaching out or seeking help started to fade because my focus turned toward finding a connection with people who understood the miserable me, instead of those who wanted to help me not be miserable any longer.

While some people will say that the desire to find similarly thinking peers is developmentally appropriate for someone in their teens, for me it manifested in an even more unhealthy relationship with self and others because of my distorted sense of self-worth, which itself was rooted in my neglected traumas and abuses. Even if the active traumas would have stopped at that point in my life, I would have continued to struggle continuously because I had no conscious idea why I was acting the way I was in the first place. Most of my self-harm began between the ages of 12 and 14. I engaged in self-cutting, suicide attempts, as well as eating changes that resulted in bouts of anorexia and bulimia. When I was alone, which was a lot of the time during these years, I destroyed property and set things on fire.

Each and every action I was taking against myself only helped fuel my self-loathing. It exacerbated my negative and risky behavior. This pattern of self-destruction became a viscous cycle and self-fulfilling prophecy at the same time. Although during this period of my life I felt utterly alone and disconnected from the experiences of everyone else, I know now from my experiences since getting healthy that I was not alone in experiencing a pattern such as this. Rather, this phenomenon is unfortunately all too common for far too many teenagers everywhere, both in the past and the present.

Being Responsible Without Being at Fault

In my work teens, I cannot count how many times I see them in emergency room situations where they have reported suicidal thoughts or suicide attempts. Some are actively engaged in cutting, drug use, or just resisting those who are trying to help them. Regardless of how they get there and despite any uniquities about specific circumstances and situations, their underlying stories are all so very similar—they have all experienced significant traumas.

Many times they recognize events and are able to verbalize at least what they have gone through, but neither the patient nor the treatment provider always recognize those situations as prior traumas that have led to the destructive behaviors that got them there.

After the initial intervention, these teenagers may end up enrolled in social services through a local behavioral health organization, but often the professionals tasked with their care are not educated to help them understand that their traumas are significant reasons for their behavioral struggles and challenges. When I speak with teens in these situations, I find that they have not connected the dots between a past sexual abuse event, divorce, or others traumas, and their suicide attempts, cutting, eating disorders, relationship difficulties, drug addictions, or life in general. No one has ever educated them that these behaviors are normal reactions to an abnormal traumatic or abusive situation.

Many of the teenagers I speak with seem to think, either because they have been outright told or had it implied, that whatever they are experiencing is their fault. That something is wrong them with them. Cutting is their fault. They are just another drug addict because they wanted to cross over the line.

I relate to these teenagers on the most fundamental levels of my being. I still remember internalizing. I remember watching the local Christian television channel for guidance. At the end of each show they told the viewers to ask for Jesus to come into their hearts and save them. I did this almost every night, hoping that when I woke up the next day He would help me be normal, and that I would no longer be a disappointment. That I would finally change.

Never once did I even know to ask for the things that were happening to me to stop. And despite my sincerest and best attempts at success, salvation was not coming through my hopes and prayers alone. Of course, it wouldn't be until much later I would understand that healing doesn't happen overnight, nor that the healing process is much more complicated and self-initiated than divine intervention on its own. I say this not to call into question religious or spiritual aspects of healing, but to reflect on how much shame and self-blame is preceded by abuse and trauma.

I assigned blame to myself. I believed I did not have the ability to help and heal myself because it was my fault. Sadly, I see this same self-doubt in the teenagers I speak with. They see themselves and the world the same as I did.

Finding the Trigger

Triggers have an enormous impact on adolescent behavior. I once worked with a young man who was becoming increasingly aggressive, withdrawing from his peers, and engaging in several very risky behaviors. His caregivers at the group home where he lived stated that these were new behaviors and that he had been acting fine until the last several weeks. I asked if there had been any changes in his lifestyle or routine, to which his case manager and caregivers both responded that there hadn't been. While I was getting ready to leave that day, I saw another person's name on the intake board who happened to have the same last name as he did. I asked the young man if he had a brother staying in the home. He said he didn't because his brother had to move out two weeks before. Somehow, neither his case manager nor caregivers thought of his brother's removal as a significant change or potential stressor for him.

Here was a child whose parents were taken away from him, and who had already experienced significant trauma during childhood that continued to influence his behavior and decision-making. Then, to top it all off, his brother suddenly disappeared, too. It does not take a PhD to connect his recent change in behavior with his triggers. Yet, his case manager and caregivers continued focusing solely be on his behavior, and not on its source.

When one of my daughters was about 12 years old, she would occasionally get upset with me when asked to do the dishes. She would end up doing them anyway, but would complete this task as slowly and with as much drama as humanly possible. Several times tempers would escalate and the dishwashing session would turn into an all-out confrontation. She would fall to the floor and start pulling out her hair. As a parent and also someone who struggled with my own self-deprecating behavior at her age, these events bothered me deeply, and I found myself struggling to properly deal with them.

I decided to do what many people do and turned to Google to research various parenting techniques. I read about positive reinforcement, structure changes, performing chores together, and other methods that focused on the behavior of her decision against doing the dishes. Nothing worked and nothing changed. She continued to do the dishes complete with drama. It was then I found myself beginning to fall into the same troubled teenager mentality of blaming the teen. As a result I began to convince myself she was hitting the age where everything was only going to get worse and not better.

Then one day it hit me like a ton of bricks. I realized that her behavior actually had nothing to do with the dishes. I realized that the behavior occurred directly after experiencing a situation that mimicked trauma she had experienced when she was only five years old. In my mind, I believed that because she wasn't currently experiencing trauma that everything was fine. I let myself believe that she couldn't have remembered anything she had experienced before the age of five, but I was dead wrong. Of course, from her perspective her behavior had nothing to do with things she couldn't consciously verbalize. She even questioned herself and her behavior, tried to change her behavior, but nothing worked until we revisited the source, the prior trauma. Once we undertook this journey together, her attitude about dishes and other facets of her life began to change and so did mine.

Not wanting to do the dishes is developmentally appropriate and something many children experience. But for my daughter, this was not the case. To compound matters, I did what many parents do and fed into her behavior instead of realizing it for the trigger it was. I am not a perfect parent after all, even with my own experiences and subsequent education. I mess up. I make mistakes. I miss things that should be obvious to me. But I am always trying to learn from my mistakes and become a better. Until I realized this trigger, I could have attempted to handle the situation any number of psychologically correct parenting ways, but the outcome would have been the same.

We must investigate red flags and respond with urgency and compassion while exploring the underlying reason for it instead of the behavior itself. In our case, the proper response was to enroll our daughter in child in counseling and work with a therapist on how to go about supporting her while she worked on it from her end. I truly believe, and am supported by trauma-informed approach that if we had focused solely on either behavior modification or just how to parent better, her behavior would have only continued to escalate. Luckily we recognized the source underlying the trigger and her behavior as a result, and we were able to intervene at an early enough stage. Because of this intervention, our daughter is able to realize and begin working through the trauma she experienced so that one day she continue on her healing path.

Note to everyone: My husband and I openly discuss my past in front of and with our children. We also discuss the events of their lives in an open manner with the intention of teaching them to live authentic lives where they don't have to hide their experiences, opinions, emotions, or the sins of others. We share a part of our family in this book with the permission of our children, and with great discretion. We do this in hopes that others will have the courage to live just as authentically. Doing so will result in less shame and blame, and more compassion and healing.

To Know and Love Thyself

A very insightful eight-year-old who experienced significant trauma, abuse and severe neglect during their short time on Earth, once told me, "I don't know how to be loved, so I act bad so people won't want to love me."

Although this admission is not usual for people to make, the experience is not at all uncommon for trauma survivors. Not knowing how to be loved, which is a byproduct of not knowing how to love oneself, stems from a distortion of self that follows trauma of all kinds. It is also something I struggled mightily with throughout my adolescence and a condition that only intensified as I entered my teenage years.

By those years, the thought that I had the words *"come rape me"* written on my forehead became louder in my head because the adults in my life were missing all the signs and symptoms my abusers keyed in on. No matter who I hung out with or where I went, I was constantly used for sex because my vulnerabilities were on open display. When I was 15, I couldn't take the pressure of being a teenager and being myself anymore, so I dropped out of school and began periodically running away. This usually happened after my mom and I had fights over curfew, cleanliness or just about anything.

During this time I also began seeking out male approval through several intimate relationships that mimicked my abuses, and eventually ended up staying at an apartment that doubled as methamphetamine lab. I hadn't experimented with drugs much prior to that period because I had a fear losing control and doing something I would regret. However, everything I was going through inside became so overwhelming that I was willing to try whatever I could to numb it. That was where the meth came in. When I was high I had the illusion of being in control and being okay, even if I was anything but that.

At the time, I never consciously thought I was addicted to the drug, but found myself very dependant on the culture and the risks inherent in the lifestyle. That's what kept me coming back. Never did I once think that I was taking drugs because my life was out of control or that it was an escape tool from dealing with my traumas, abuses and absence of love of self. Everything started to happen so fast, and soon the only thing that mattered was what was going on in that moment—doing the drugs and running further away from what got me there in the first place.

During this time I was estranged from my parents, and burning any bridges remaining with pretty much everyone who stood by me through my adolescent years. Because of this, I buried myself deeper in my new relationships. People finally wanted to be around me, they laughed at my jokes and trusted me with information. We hung out for days on end, like family just having a great time together. I think that these connections, as unhealthy as they were, kept me coming back just as much, if not more so, than the drugs. I also know that the people I met during this time were mostly decent at heart. They were just there to bury something inside of themselves they could not deal with either; with the drugs and the lifestyle we were engaged in acting as the dirt and shovels. This togetherness would not last. The lab was eventually raided and those of us who did not get arrested went our separate ways.

Shortly after the breakup, I made my way into a shelter that was also an independent living program. I had my own apartment, and was working full time while also taking GED classes, which I enjoyed. The shelter served people under 18 only. Some of the residents had children of their own and some didn't. I had a lot of independence, few rules, and I didn't run the risk of getting kicked out for messing up. It was a good place for me to be at the time, and I was getting on my feet again as well as making some good choices for the first time in a while. I received valuable life-education skills including budgeting, cooking classes and résumé classes.

It worked well for a while on some levels, but during that time I continued engaging in some risky behaviors, like meeting guys on Internet chat lines. My inability to adequately judge an unhealthy or unsafe situation and relationship for what it was had not changed, even though my atmosphere had. My inability to understand the impact my traumas and abuses had on my judgment, combined with my inability to love myself due to those traumas, resulted in unhealthy and unsafe interactions with men of all kinds. With the rise in children using the Internet, this type of risky behavior has become even more prevalent among pre-teens and teens now than it was then.

Recently there have been news stories about parents who publicly shame their children through the vehicle of the Internet upon catching their underage daughters online pretending to be older, and carrying on sexually explicit contact of some sort with older men. Many other parents chime in to praise or chastise these parents for holding their children accountable. Yet no one seems to be asking the tough and even uncomfortable questions about why those children feel the need to act in such a manner in the first place.

More often than not, children do not engage in such behaviors because they woke up one day and decided they wanted to risk their lives by treating themselves as sexual objects.

Some people blame the media and television for this behavior, but there are plenty of children who watch the same shows and do not act out in this manner.

No, it is very easy to blame society, and even easier to blame the children themselves, but for some of those children, the culprit is something deep down inside that happened to them at some point(s) in their lives, and is now manifesting as risky and inappropriate sexualized behaviors. These behaviors replace a love of self those children do not know how to foster, with lust of traumatic expression run amok. Let's take a look at some of the ways trauma can manifest in the behavior patterns of teenagers, in order to understand that sometimes these actions are cries for help covering up traumas and abuses:

- Running away
- Suicide attempts
- Self-harm
- Eating disorders
- Risky behaviors, including sexual activity
- Cruelty to animals
- Low self-esteem
- Aggressive behavior
- Drug use
- Mental health problems
- Helping the Whole Person

Some teenagers have proactive people in their lives that try to get them help, yet many interventions don't work because the focus is on the behavior and not the symptoms, or the diagnosis and not the person. Especially when working with teens, I have heard many parents and caregivers express this about their kids:

We have been seeing so and so counselor for x number of years or months but it doesn't seem to be helping

We have tried x number of medications and we have had x number of side-effects, and every time they change his or her medications it takes several months to settle

We have set up an intake but it takes two to three months for an assessment, so we switched from our old provider because things weren't working

The reason these well-meaning interventions do not work is because all of them deal primarily with the behavior, the surface, the diagnosis and the stigma attached to it all. These routes focus on behavior modification and specifically with a child's life in the present only. In the behavioral healthcare field by and large, the focus largely remains on the diagnosis and the medication prescription and therapy to treat that diagnosis in the here and now only.

This is one of the largest shortcomings of the mental health field, although we are beginning to see some positive changes. Many remain stuck in the past, even though they are well-intentioned. Their training focuses them on treating the behavior before them instead of the roots beneath, the entire person. This refusal to look back at what might have caused the manifestation of behavioral symptoms long before any symptoms existed is something that is still marginalized and ignored in behavioral care. I'm happy to see that the trauma-informed is beginning to make some in-roads.

We owe it to our children to move away from the surface approach. We owe it to them to work on providing more comprehensive, holistic and compassionate care. We owe it to them to withhold judgment and blame. We owe it to them to work together in order to begin doing better at taking the time to find the source of their issues instead of furthering covering them up. We have to help them to either learn or re-learn to love themselves from the inside out, which is the only way true healing and happiness can ever take place. We have to, because their lives and their futures depend on it.

CHAPTER 6

Healing and Overcoming Trauma

By my adulthood, every part of who I was and what I did incurred some sort of societal stigma and label describing it. I was the homeless girl wandering the streets, the addict sucking off the system, the prostitute, the smelly girl with no teeth, the person sleeping on the bus you avoided, and the list went on and on. The sustained suppression of all my traumas combined with a lack of resources and support to help me understand them resulted in a person who was one step from death on the outside, while feeling so very dead on the inside. So much so that the outside was simply following suit.

I wished for my life to magically transform itself into something better overnight, but the next day was no different than the one before it. It kept repeating itself and the cycle continued until I finally was able to take a long, hard and painful look at myself to see that the change had to come from within, and that it was not going to be a quick or easy fix.

Or, in the wise words of the amazing FLY LADY, an online support blogger helping many like myself: "This mess didn't happen overnight and it is not going to get better overnight, so let's take it one day at a time." Because of the work I have done, my life is what I always wished for it to be. In the end I had to make it happen. Once motivated toward healing, I gladly accepted help from people who understood I was much more than any labels, stigmas, behaviors or actions.

The old interventions and self-help tactics didn't work for me. They weren't responsible for my transformation. Neither were the many programs preaching social conformity and the shame, silence and submission that many times more than not accompanies them. I could never find peace inside when I was being sold a bill of goods telling me peace would come if I could become something other people wanted me to be.

My transformation began when I let go of the shame and stigmas I held onto so tightly and that went down so deeply for such a long time. It was a lot of hard, frightening and uncomfortable work, but it forced me to understand and heal my life, my family systems, and myself.

Did I mention it was frightening? At first it was very much so. I found that I was afraid of everything. Although it makes me laugh now, back then I feared that I would transform into a suburbanite and become the Better Homes and Gardens version of normal. I thought that my husband was never going to deal with his issues and that would affect our relationship. I worried that I would repeat the vicious cycle I had fallen into time and time again, which would only continue to hurt my children and myself. The fear was based on all of this and more. It wasn't easy, but I can say without the slightest bit of reserve or hesitation, that facing and fixing my inner demons was the best decision I have ever made. The process tested me in ways I didn't know were possible, but as I learned more about myself I have been able to let go of so much hate for the people who hurt me or failed to protect me—and myself.

People see me differently now. I am respected for my success as well as my willingness and ability to help others by sharing my experiences. I enjoy engaging in life-altering discussions that help enlighten and empower people. My support system helps me to be happy and healthy instead of the sick and stuck person I was back then.

I might look, act and even think much differently than I did then, but let me be clear: My worth today is no different than it was 15 years ago. I have always been worthy, and I have always deserved the healthy love I receive today. The difference between then and now simply exists in my understanding of this fact. Although I sometimes wish I could have loved and valued myself from the beginning, I also realize that only by overcoming the labels, stigmas and struggles, am I able to be the person I am today.

Helping Others Heal

We see the effects of trauma across the spectrum. Trauma has no boundaries. It doesn't know socioeconomic, cultural, ideological or ethnic boundaries. And it is far past time for us, all of us, regardless of any manufactured differences we have, to come together and deal with it. We have discussed throughout this book what trauma is, what it looks like, and how it affects people in various ways, but what about all of this can we actually change?

The answer to this question is actually quite simple, even though the road is fraught with convoluted paths. The ACE's Study gives us a simple step toward this answer. Validating prior research, it showed that children who bond with at least one caring adult are more likely to overcome the lasting effects of adversity.

In my experience, it was the healthy and caring people I bonded with who are as much of the reason I survived and now thrive, as anything I have done myself. When the storms raged, I had a strong foundation to hold onto because of those relationships. So how then do we become that caring adult?

Caring Adults

Preventing trauma would erase the need for trauma-informed therapy altogether. Wouldn't that be nice? But the news reminds us every night that we have a long way to go. In the meantime we need to be aware and informed. We need to be caring adults.

So what should a caring adult look like from a child's perspective? They are neither perfect nor unflinching authoritarians. They:

- are open and honest

- care for the child's best interest

- withhold judgment and blame

- allow a child to make decisions, but offer advice and guidance when requested or when necessary

- set limits and provide boundaries

A cared-for child knows that without a doubt, that even when they make a mistake, they can come to a caring adult for guidance. That child can call them on their good and bad days alike, and even if sometimes they choose not to call, the caring adult will still be there for them. A caring adult knows that it's not about their own biases, fears, norms and values, but about the child's growth and betterment despite these limitations.

This is a picture of the safe, caring adults in my life. These were the only people I allowed into my life then, and the only ones I allow in my life and my children's lives now. Safe people come in all sorts of lifestyles, professions and personality types.

I have a friend whose safe people were strict and would reign her in if needed. She responded well to this kind of feedback and even respected them for the way they went about setting their ground rules and enforcing their boundaries. They were a good match.

One of my favorite aunts told me that one of her grandsons said, "Your house is my favorite home to go to. It has the most rules, but I also have the most fun here." It should be stated here that many people mistake structure with control. Having structure is good, and it helps young people grow into responsible, accountable and self-sufficient people. However, when someone who structures choices for others based on biases, stereotypes or beliefs in order to manipulate or indoctrinate them into that person's lifestyle, that is control.

Being a safe and proactive person should not end with just helping individual children. Rather, we should be working to create a caring community environment, complete with social systems that ensure safety, security and success for every child. I've had the opportunity to work with various organizations and programs designed for survivors of sexual exploitation. When looking at the services many of these organizations provide, their structure primarily stresses and mandates the restriction of personal freedom. They facilitate programs from a fear- and shame-based perspective, which is ironically similar to the protocol for abusive relationships.

In domestic violence situations, people are shamed and scared into constantly revisiting unhealthy and unsafe relationships with the person suppressing their will. Despite the best intention of many programs that vow to fight such situations, a lot of people end up washing out due to this fear and shame-based agenda. These people then end up back with their abusers, using substances—and in the case of human trafficking, back to their trafficker or the streets.

Putting Trauma Victims First

Many policies and laws having to do with child protection and juvenile delinquency are formed by people who believe they are best positioned to create them because they've never experienced the traumas that put kids in these situations. Kids are doubly victimized at the hands of policymakers with good intentions. But the truth of the matter is that those in charge have had very different lives than those who have experienced trauma.

Many times politicians and others who enact legislation overseeing trauma and abuse sufferers have never ever taken time to talk with a trauma survivor or someone in the situation they are making laws and policies for. There is a big difference between working with trusted, vested and compassionate allies versus working with people involved in a movement. In movements, survivors are often used as nothing more than public relations' tokens that serve to further a social, political or economic agenda. Survivors are there to smile for the cameras, but not valued nor respected for their ideas and perspectives.

In order to create a safer and more trauma-centered approach that works, we have to start thinking and acting with more than just our uninformed perspectives of what survivors need in order to get better. Here are a few places to start:

- Survivors are not just their stories or stigmas. We have a lot to offer outside of experiences with whatever trauma or abuse we have experienced. It is so important to keep this at the forefront of your mind whether you are working on policies or running an organization that provides direct services to survivors

- Don't ever say, "This is OUR survivor" when you introduce a person. Their purpose is not to serve your organization through their experiences. When we use phrases and mannerisms like this, we are doing nothing more than cementing them as tokens

- Do ask people who have been in similar situations for advice, and don't discount their opinions simply because they don't fit within the norms and values of the way business has always been done

- Please do not patronize or treat survivors as children. They have been treated this way their entire lives, and that treatment is a huge part of their struggles thus far

- Supporting and celebrating accomplishments is important, but be careful not to act shocked or in disbelief that a survivor has accomplished something. Also, please don't speak slowly and simply to us, as we are not stupid just because we are struggling

- Children who have experienced exploitation feel and act years beyond their current age. It is not about taking them back to ages they lost, but moving forward with them from where they currently are

- Having a survivor involved in everyday decisions and leadership roles is crucial, but don't expect every survivor to want to join a crusade and help other victims. It should never be an expectation but rather a non-judgmentally, respected personal decision

- Trust that survivors are just as competent and capable as you are in every way, shape and form. How can we expect someone to trust us if we don't trust them?

Note to Survivors: Your accomplishments and successes are yours and yours alone. People may walk with you through and assist you in your journey, love you, support you, and have a huge impact on your life. However, at the end of the day it is the work you have done that earned your accomplishments. You have dug deep and faced whatever it is that you have needed to face, and continue to do so. No one, whether it is a person or an organization, should take credit for the success you bred within and around yourself.

When providing services in any capacity, it is essential to have an array of programs and offerings that meet the needs of both individuals and the community. During my degree program we were presented with various scenarios of clients as case studies. During instruction, every one of our introductions would refer to Alcoholics Anonymous when speaking about addictions services, without ever mentioning or considering that this approach might not be the right fit for everyone. Now let me preface this by saying I am a fan of twelve-step programs. I just want to make it clear that there is a need for a variety of services, and not just a one-size-fits-all template.

In my interactions with various organizations and clinical professionals, there is a prevalent ideology stating that if someone doesn't want to go to rehab or through one of these programs where they are pressured to admit shame, helplessness and powerlessness, then they don't want help at all. What these professionals forget is that the people make the program, and not the steps. If you are willing to look inside of yourself for the answers you seek, have a great support system around you, surround yourself with non-judgmental people who model healthy behaviors and set healthy boundaries, the results of your decisions will be undoubtedly positive. That kind of healthy living and doing will be what fills the current gaps in communities seeking to help people in these sorts of situations—not just stoic and static stepped processes as has been considered the benchmark standard in the past.

We have to be very careful to not facilitate the replacement of one addiction for another with these sorts of stepped self-help programs. When the root of the issue that causes a behavior like drug and alcohol use is not addressed, many people end up replacing their original addictive behaviors with whatever the program isn't addressing. In many twelve-step programs, this switch includes the reliance upon nicotine and caffeine among other behavioral modifiers. However, just because the person quit his or her original addition in no way means they are healed or fixed. Obviously, there are still ongoing issues related to the trauma that are not addressed and are usually the reason for relapse.

For example, if you were physically and sexually abused as a child and started using drugs as a way to cope, you might struggle with drugs on and off, go to rehab a few times, and then decide you want to stay clean and sober for several years. You cut out all your old friends and start having various successes. Maybe you start school, get a real job, make amends, and start feeling really good. From a surface perspective, this means you have been fixed, right? Then something happens to trigger a memory of what led to your self-destructive behaviors in the first place, but because you never dealt with the core issue things turn back to bad quickly.

Maybe you get back in contact with an unhealthy family member or friend, or you get stuck in another unhealthy relationship. Maybe the circumstances are different this time, but the outcome ends up being the same, and leaves you back at the original starting point or even worse. All because the core issue never was recognized and amended, so no deep healing could ever take place. All of the surface measures you took were no match for the core issue once it came back to the surface, and once it did you are back where you began.

Triggers in Rehabilitation

Triggers within addiction surround the "who" and "what" questions. People are told that triggers are the people they got high with or the places they went so they should recognize those triggers and stay away. This is a good start but there are other triggers that probably have more of an impact on people than running into an old friend at the store. In fact, a case can easily be made that we are the company we keep based upon what is going on inside of us, which then manifests on the outside into our relationships with others. You might not have been friends with that person in the first place depending on whether or not you were healthy and happy inside of yourself.

The triggers most likely to affect people are going to be related to their past and to the trauma they have experienced. If a person experienced severe neglect as a child and that person is clean and doing well, but then someone who they believe is a caring person ends up rejecting them, they're likely to be triggered. Not the person doing the rejecting mind you, but the behavior, which results in the rehashing of unpleasant experiences one has not properly recognized, understood or dealt with.

Within programs and shelters we have the honor to work with someone for a short time: three to six months typically. It becomes easy for us to think that because our client has made tremendous progress, like staying clean or not talking to their abuser during that time, they are going to transition back into society problem-free. This represents the "who" and "what" mentality mentioned earlier.

As providers, we also must look at the services someone is receiving, and the "why" behind their success. With typical services, a person has a case manager, a structured program to follow, a counselor, basic life skills, and involvement in various support groups. The program usually has an intended life span of approximately six month along with many attached stipulations including job searching, attendance and adherence measured by means including drug testing.

In many cases, these programs appear very successful. Often it's because a person is isolated from his or her triggers during its duration. However when they graduate and are back on their own, they are thrust into a world full of potential triggers. Healing doesn't happen overnight, and if all someone got out of a program was a GED, a few classes on budgeting, and a cookie-cutter structure of what healthy relationships should look like, all the progress made is still only surface fodder for the arduous road ahead. Because this program might not have helped the person recognize and understand the root causes of their triggers and subsequent struggles, all successes remain at risk of significant setbacks when and if the triggers connected to those issues come to light again.

Successfully Measuring Success

So where do these programs go wrong and how can we make them better? Success should be measured by integrated and qualitative change, rather than quantitative data that measures how many hours, classes or items a person logged while in a shelter setting. Often this is not simply a program issue, but rather a top-down executive one. Funders often want to see measurable and empirically tangible results, like completing a GED. A successful program equates to high GED completion rates, successful job placement, and college or technical school enrollment.

Let's face it. We live in a very outcome oriented society. We are taught through education, advertising and the media that the product or outcome is far more important than the process or journey to get there—or that the ends justify the means each and every time. This future time orientation results in many of the policies in place today.

The majority of these boardroom conversations consist of how to meet the tangible and quantitative goals. This includes the employment of other surface programs like adding transportation and childcare services. This is because the prevalent belief is that convenience equals success. Don't get me wrong, all of these factors are important to the success of individuals within a program. But if we want to change lives, we also have to change the conversation from the surface to something deeper, more meaningful and permanent. We have to get down to the root. To help discuss how to do so, the following ideas should be considered the minimum baseline requirement when working with clients:

- They should receive psycho education centering on the effects of trauma and abuse. This should not be limited to healthy relationships or parenting classes. Showing clients the cycle of abuse is not enough, they must be provided with new skills and ways to recognize, understand and begin to heal

- If a program is running groups for life skills, such as budgeting, think big picture. What is poverty? How do systemic issues like institutional racism or sexism affect your client's access to care and everyday life? Share this information with your clients so that they can begin to comprehend the larger forces and interests shaping society and their place in it. Don't simply give them a tool like budgeting, congratulate them on a good job, and then complain to your co-workers about a having to teach a budgeting class, you're your clients have no money to budget. Talk about the many ways your clients may struggle and really look into the reasons why. We shouldn't be afraid to talk to clients about real issues like race, class, or gender inequalities. These are the issues that affect them and all of us directly, and won't disappear when they transition out of services.

- Programs should integrate clients and the community, whether it is through a shelter or a mentoring program. One of my great friends and mentors Celestia Tracy said, "Abuse happens in the community, so healing must happen in community."

- There is such a thing as too many services. Remember, most abuse involves some form of control, so if our services mimic control, we will push clients away. This is not because they don't want the help or are not ready to change, but rather because in their perspective the new system is just as restrictive as the old one

- Your clients are not cases—they are human beings! A case implies something to be managed and compartmentalized. Calling our clients "cases" can be felt as degrading and insulting from their perspectives. Call them clients, call them people, call them human beings, but leave the word case to mean what you carry your files to and from the office in, or where you store your books at home.

The most successful programs I have witnessed are low-barrier, choice-driven, supportive, client-centered and non-judgmental. Success is measured through a matrix of tangible and intangible factors, stretching far beyond whether or not a client graduates the program. Programs that can successfully utilize their community supports when and if they are in trouble or need a connection to further services. A program is successful when its clients feel safe and comfortable, while truly knowing the individuals there are people they can turn to. You are successful when your clients continue to have support throughout their journey, even if they are no longer sitting directly in front of you. This means they have not just learned a life skill like cooking, but also a much more important one like how to be an advocate for themselves.

Finally, remember that people receiving services should not have to conform to what we feel is best for them. Shelters and twelve-step programs are not always the only or best solutions in every case. We have to offer choices of supportive, client-centered services that meet the needs of our clients and the community they call home. We need to make sure our services meet people where they are at, rather than making them feel inferior for not being where and who we think it is they need to be.

The Perception of Normalcy

There was a point in my life where I behaved erratically, like putting a can of Pepsi in the microwave and turning it on "just because". My brain was in constant turmoil. I had intrusive thoughts about death and rape every 10 to 15 minutes throughout the day and night. I had visions of car crashes and my children being raped in front of me periodically. It was something terrible to think about, but was just something I lived with. I didn't know these thoughts were abnormal nor did I consciously understand the effect they had on my everyday life.

Again, success at that time was being clean, not getting raped and not beating my children. If I could go from dawn to dusk accomplishing all of that, then I was considered normal.

There also came a time when I immediately stopped taking all of the psych medications I was prescribed and I became determined to just be better at life. This was not a popular decision with those I was receiving services from but one that I made for myself because I knew it was the right thing to do. It made sense to me. Around this same time, I found a love for photography, which helped me more than any pill I took ever did.

Being behind the lens of a camera was the only thing that ever helped my mind settle down. When I was shooting or editing, my mind couldn't wonder and I would have no intrusive, offensive or frightening thoughts. Just being able to have periodic breaks from the chaos going on within my head really started to help me focus, and to look forward to something that enriched and empowered me. It was also the first thing outside of my marriage and my children I was proud of.

Photography gave me the courage to get my GED and start college. By no means did I overcome everything through my photography, but it played an integrally and fundamentally important role in the overall process. I have heard similar stories from many survivors—whether it is yoga, meditation, cooking, painting, working on cars, fixing things, or whatever else enriches someone's life. For some people it is journaling, writing, drawing, or music. Even today if I am having a stressful moment, I can always unwind by being behind the lens. I write this to remind you why we need a variety of programs. I have never met anyone with a recovery story just like mine, or like anyone else's for that matter. We are all individual and healing must be individualized or else we risk focusing on conformity and submission, versus empowerment, enlightenment and the integration of long lasting, meaningful and healthful change.

Walk through the journey beside your kids, beside your clients.

So let's recap some of those crucial moments and realizations in my journey of healing:

• First and foremost was safety. Even though I was hyper-sexualized, over-stimulated and having constant body responses to trauma, I was safe. I had food in my belly, a roof over my head, and a few people I felt safe talking to

• My relationships were not perfect but were safe

- Discovering photography helped my brain settle down enough to allow change to happen

- I was able to start thinking ahead a little, and see past just that minute, hour or day

- I passed my GED and started to have my own successes, as well as doing things that enriched and empowered me

- I started connecting with other people at school, getting close with instructors, and as a result my community of support began expanding

- I started to learn more about the meanings underlying my thoughts and beliefs, and as a result how to advocate for myself. I actually had a lot of skills sets from the streets that helped me to do this. I was great at finding resources and connecting with people because that's how I survived. I learned to channel these skills in a healthy way

- I found that fateful link on Facebook, which finally gave a name and identity to my trauma. This allowed me to tell my story for the first time, which validated the horrors I'd survived

- I received trauma counseling that was set at my own pace

- My community started to grow exponentially and more positive connections were made, so that I now have people to talk to and process with even though I no longer officially, actively receive services

The benchmarks should be how we measure results and success within a shelter, behavioral health, counseling or rehabilitation setting. As you can see, some of these benchmarks are quantitative, such as my GED, but others are qualitative, including learning more about the meaning of my thoughts and beliefs. Just because the GED can be measured on a scale and my thoughts cannot, in no way makes the GED more important. In fact, if I did not have the periods of qualitative introspection, then quantitative accomplishments like my GED and college diploma would not have been possible.

The most important foundation for anyone is safety. The goal should not be based on our definitions of how to make people feel safe in their environment. Rather, it should be about what safety means to the person needing it and how we can work on creating it with and for them based on their combined thoughts, efforts and energies. Meeting basic needs is a fantastic step in creating safety, but it is not the only component.

This is why structured shelter, housing and rehabilitation models work so well for some people at first, but when people leave and feel unsafe again, they relapse into old or new behaviors stemming from their trauma.

Safety is not just getting away from your abuser; safety comes from having a sense of security, awareness of self, and efficacy in one's self, too. If we want our programs and people to be successful, we need to stop measuring success based on the amount of services offered—and start measuring based on how well we make individuals feel safe and loved, as well as how we help them learn to love and therefore, help themselves.

Conclusion

I want to preface this last section by stating that this is not a self-help book. I tried those and they didn't work because individuals need community in order to heal. None of the progress I've made would have been possible if it was not for my own healing first. I became a social worker because of my trauma. I have remained a social worker because I have healed. My parenting choices, the way I see the world, my commitment to improving my relationships and not being judgmental of others, all came from the processes that I went through to overcome my own junk. I am going to talk about the things in my life that I do differently and see differently with my own children, family, and community than the individuals in my life did. The understanding given to me by becoming a social worker has created the lasting change I was desperately searching for and the freedom I desired but couldn't find.

Some things that we can do with our children that are key to helping them feel comfortable telling us if something ever does happen is by talking about sexual abuse and appropriate touch, casually and openly. Here are some guidelines:

- We should talk about it often. We also should talk about consent, what "no" means, and why, even if someone is being tickled and they ask you stop, it is important to listen and respect their "no". We should never force our kids to hug or kiss anyone they don't want to. As much as we possibly can remember we should teach them to ask, "Can/may I have a hug/snuggle?"

- We should use appropriate terms for all body parts.

- I try to explain the effects of abuse to my kids in age appropriate terms. For instance, with the little ones I say, "You know how if you fall down and get a scrape you can see the cut or bruise? Well if someone touches your penis or vagina, or shows you their penis or vagina, it can hurt your heart and your brain, even though you may not see the marks."

- We should talk to our kids about trauma and abuse. With my older kids, we talk openly about everything and when we talk about abuse or trauma. We talk about the negative effects it has on someone's life, but also that while it is not 100 percent preventable. It is 100 percent overcome-able. I truly believe that.

- We should teach kids to not only stand up for their own bodies but for others as well. In my family, this has helped because they all watch out for each other and pay attention to their siblings.

- We should talk to them about paying attention to their "creeper vibe." If something makes them feel uncomfortable or icky in their stomach, my kids know they can tell us even if they don't think it is a big deal. Believe me, they do. If someone brushes up against their butt while walking, they will tell us.

- We should be extra vigilant to know where and with whom our kids are having sleepovers. While we do not stop our kids from having sleepovers, we do talk to them every time they are going to be somewhere without us about dangers and what to do. We pay attention to who they stay with and if we see signs of abuse in the kids or in the home, then we don't allow them to stay, but also don't stop them from playing with them, either. That just causes isolation and does no one any good shutting the door for further conversations.

- We should show our kids examples of healthy touch. In our relationship, my husband and I show examples of healthy consensual touch. My husband does not objectify women in any way and loves and supports me. He supports and loves our kids for exactly who they are and who they want to be.

Note to Survivors: I was incredibly hyper-sexualized as a child. I made everything about sex in my jokes and in my conversations, but when it came to expressing my desires or needs in a bedroom, or even giving consent, I would shut down. Being sexual is not bad at all and you should enjoy the sex you are having or be able to not have it if you so choose. For me, it was more about finding my worth in sex. I felt like the only way I could be loved was by having sex, and I would have whatever sex anybody wanted to make them happy. I had absolutely no boundaries or choices or desires of my own. Luckily, at the time that I needed it the most my husband/partner was very safe, talked to me about how I was feeling, and as time progressed, I was able to own my sexuality and learn my own body. That came from being in a safe relationship, therapy, and processing with my husband. It is still a work in progress, and that's okay. I am supported and nothing has to change overnight.

The way each family should handle this topic is unique to each family's situation. The way I handled it would be different if, for instance, my husband and I divorced like my parents did when I was little. I would recognize that the divorce, no matter how clean, leaves the child vulnerable during that time and during the transition. It would be important for me to increase my awareness of our new surroundings, talk to my kids about what is going on, how they are feeling, and encourage them to be extra mindful of their surroundings and their gut feelings.

Creating a Safe Environment

I'm honest with my kids about everything. Sometimes I think I am speaking great words of wisdom and all they hear is Mrs. Donavan from Charlie Brown. Then they do something or say something that makes my heart melt and I know we are not total screw-ups. I still get the "ugh not again" or in my case, "Mom, I am going to a friend's house. Please don't social work their family." Yet, they are all little advocates who fight for others. We are not perfect—I wouldn't want us to be. I want our kids to see us mess up and overcome things.

I have noticed there are a few things my kids have that are important to their feeling of safety; these are the types of thing we can recreate in our communities and programs for kids:

- They have groups of core friends. Even if they fight and bicker, they have friends that they can remember from previous years and are still connected with.

- They have stability.

- They are involved in extracurricular activities. It is not about keeping them busy, but about connecting them with safe, caring adults who they can trust. They have access to other safe, caring adults that they can talk to and learn from.

- If, God forbid, something happens to them, they know they have family and community support that would be there for them.

- We don't shy away from talking about real issues and are pretty open and honest about our lives and our mess-ups. They know can talk to us about these things and others. My kids are not afraid to talk about their feelings and they make amazing self-reflective connections that blow me away sometimes.

- They have a team of teachers that support them in the classroom and encourage them outside of the classroom.

- My kids are not hyper-sexualized but are able to talk about sex and ask questions. My kids are not afraid to speak their mind and are not living in constant fear. Even though we have struggled financially, they have always had their basic needs met.

- Above all, my kids are able to be exactly who they want to be. We have rules and expectations, but their choices are theirs and what they want to be or do is their choice.

There are still times when children won't disclose even if we have best practices in place. This doesn't mean the abuse hasn't happened. I'm going to share two contrasting stories that will show how we can handle abuse and recovery in the home or out of the home in case a child was placed or is living in a program.

When I six I was raped by my teenage cousin, and his stepdad came into the room afterwards and saw that something inappropriate was going on. If you remember from earlier in the book he said, "I won't tell your mom if you promise never to do it again." This was detrimental to my psyche and left me incredibly vulnerable because it wasn't addressed right away and safety wasn't ensured. I was never able to talk about it until years later and had a lot of instability with very few lasting safe adult relationships as a result.

At the same tender age of six, one of my children was exposed to pornography on a smartphone. They didn't tell me when it happened because of the shame and fear of getting in trouble. We had no idea it had happened until one day we found all sorts of porn on our computer. It was very hardcore and something no child should be exposed to. When we talked to them about it, they were very upset and didn't want to talk about it. We assured them that they were not in trouble and that we just wanted to make sure they were safe and that we just wanted to know how they found it. They told us the entire story. They had been exposed on a smartphone about two weeks prior, it was more of something that they happened upon based on a search. This exposure led to them searching specifics on a Google search. It was a huge leap for one week and took us completely by surprise. I talk to my kids about everything and I have talked to my kids about porn, but never thought that conversation would have to happen as early as body safety conversations.

In this case it was okay for me to dig deeper and ask questions because there did not appear to be an outside party that exposed them. If this had been a possible molestation or rape, I would have needed to have contacted police and get them in for a forensic interview through a local family advocacy center.

We sat down as a family and talked to our child about it in a calm, non-threatening way. From my perspective I told them that it would hurt their heart and head just like if someone touched their penis or vagina. We asked if it felt "wrong" or "gave a feelings in their stomach," and they said yes. My husband explained that it is important to pay attention to that feeling and if you get that feeling to come talk to mommy or daddy. I took the "we want to protect you" side and my husband took the "accountability" side. We talked about how important it is not to show other kids what they saw because it would hurt their brains and hearts, too.

Note to Readers: Sexual abuse has a domino effect. Exposure to pornography at a young age like this is absolutely sexual abuse. It will cause changes in behavior, acting out what they see, aggression and addiction to pornography, and compulsive masturbation. It can also have other effects like change in mood, depression, self-harm, and so on.

We were very proactive over the next few weeks watching for other changes in behaviors, not scheduling any play dates or sleepovers, and making sure to be extra mindful. My other kids were also mindful and would talk to us about anything that was said or done that may have been out of the norm. After about two weeks we had another incident, different this time; they had taken some pictures to imitate what they saw the weeks before. Our conversation again was calm and non-threatening. We had a very similar conversation about the feeling you get in your tummy and how it could it can hurt your brain and heart, and how other people can see pictures without you even knowing it. This time we added that we knew this was something they were thinking about because of what they saw, and that it didn't mean anything was wrong with them. We told them that if they were thinking about it they could come talk to us to and we would talk about it.

We were cautious and had a plan that if we had another incident or sign, like bedwetting or significant behavior changes, we would take them to counseling. We also talked to the school counselor and had the teachers watch for changes in behavior or in their art. I called some of my friends who are mentors and psychologists and processed through with them if they thought I was handling the situation correctly, and just to decompress because it was triggering, probably because my child was the same age as I was when I first experienced sexual abuse.

Our conversations with our child were calm, but I had to leave the room when I found out, process it a bit, cry, and think through the best way to handle the situation before we talked to our child about it. It is okay to be upset and angry, and it is okay to express your feelings to your child just as long as it doesn't make them feel the blame. For example I said, "This is hard for mommy because it makes me worried that you could get hurt if we don't talk about it. Mommy wants to keep you safe and things like this can make us unsafe."

It may seem extreme for us to involve other people and talk to their teachers about something so "uncomfortable," but as their parent it is my responsibility to not only keep my children as safe as I can but also to prevent the domino effect. If we didn't take the steps that we took, it may have spread. That's how it works; we see this in families and communities. One person is sexually abused and then they act out on the next person who repeats the pattern.

A dear friend of mine had a beautiful example of healing out of the most unimaginable experience. She had been married and had four children after getting out of a situation very similar to mine. She felt that she had a good life because she had a nice house, a good car, and was involved in her church and her kid's activities. Her childhood was one of control through religion and she was always striving for the image of perfection. She didn't really see this as abuse and felt that her life was stable. There were definitely unhealthy behaviors and parenting mistakes she was making but they didn't appear to be too detrimental. She recognizes them now that she is out of the situation, but she couldn't when she was neck deep. She was striving for the image of perfection that she was taught growing up, and didn't see the warning signs of the horrific reality she was about to find going on under her own roof.

Fortunately, and extremely bravely, one of her daughters came forward and disclosed that her father had been sexually abusing her and her sister. There was lot to the story, but basically she had to start from scratch and work on mending her family and begin the process of healing from her entire history. Her children needed counseling but she knew the only way she could best support them through the process was to get her own counseling; not just to get help parenting children who had experienced abuse and trauma, but to get help with her own childhood and the abusive marriage she was in. Without doing that first, she would not have be able to make the positive decisions she had to and most likely the communication between her and her kids would not be what it is today.

Doing Your Own Work

This same friend and I often do training together on the importance of trauma work.. Even though we didn't have the same experiences, we applied what have gained through our own healing (which looked different for both us) and found the outcomes to be the same: positive, open, supportive relationships with our children that have broken a cycle of abuse. Our lives aren't perfect, but our kids, despite all of our experiences, are thriving in their environments and I have to believe that comes from us doing our own work first.

So what does doing you own work look like? One of my biggest pet peeves during my social work program was that we were always told, "In the airplane, why do they say to put the mask on yourself first? Because if you can't breathe, you can't help your child breathe." It is a great analogy and it is so true; the problem is that we are told to take care of ourselves first and to only practice self-care. We are told to run, exercise, eat healthy, meditate, get enough sleep, don't bring the work home, and make time for our families and ourselves. This is great advice for people who haven't experienced trauma, but the problem is that most people get into helping professions because of their own life experiences or those of a close friend or family member.

One of the most important things programs need to remember is that their workers are people too, with their own pasts and issues. That is why it is so important for helping professions to require their workers to do a year of their own counseling while in the program. I wouldn't have got nearly as much out of my program if I weren't doing my own counseling while in it. Self-care alone is not enough; it's not effective when you are still in survival mode or being triggered.

If you do seek counseling or begin to work on you own trauma, here are some tips on how to advocate for your own healing:

• One of the things that helped me the most was a timeline.

When you are working with a therapist, if they don't have you make one ask them to work on one with you.

- You can get second opinions. If you were diagnosed with a disease and weren't getting care that was working, you would seek a second opinion. You should do that with a therapist, too.

- It takes time to build a therapeutic relationship, but you should feel comfortable with your therapists.

- Community is extremely important and connecting with others who have been there can be helpful.

- Keep pushing forward. Even if you have a bad experience with a helping professional, it does not mean there is no one out there that is a good fit.

- Talk about your boundaries and if you have reservations about medications express that.

- Coping skills are very important but should not be the only thing worked on. If you're not getting an understanding of the relationship between your trauma and behaviors, you need to talk with your therapists. There might be reasons you haven't gone there yet, or they may refer you to someone who specializes in trauma.

One of the curriculums that helped me the most through my healing was a workbook called Mending The Soul (Zondervan). It is a faith-based curriculum that helped me understand trauma, name my abuse, and understand how it affected my life. Again, though there were an array of services and events that helped me heal, what really made a difference was having other people around me who had done their own work and who in turn supported me. Working with a trauma therapist and a mentor were also vital in my success.

This process looks different for everyone, but be careful to not take on too much at one time. Healing is hard work, and for the first while it is like having a full-time job. Don't try to change everything at once; let it happen organically. It doesn't have to be all about goals like quitting smoking; celebrate the fact that you have gone several days without thinking negatively or that you made a huge discovery about yourself. Those are all successes, and while they might not be measurable to others, they are still huge successes for you.

Sometimes despite our best efforts, we are not in a safe place and things around us are not conducive to our goals. I talked a lot about creating safety in programs and services. It is important, but don't feel that because you are not in an ideal situation that you can't still move forward. A good friend of mine was in a horribly abusive, oppressive relationship. Obviously, at that time she was not safe, but I couldn't expect her to just leave or try to convince her to do so. Instead, we talked often, and throughout the process I reassured her that everything she was feeling and normal and we would just simply process through things. She started to work with therapists, and found that one of the things that was important for her was continuing to have conversations with the people who supported her. Eventually, she felt safe and strong enough to make her own decisions about when, where, and how to leave. The change was created for her and by her. Her recovery and choices have been much different than if someone had told her or forced her to get out, and yet her growth has been lasting. Even though she has bad days, she has come incredibly far and is rocking her life. She did it her own way, and that is what integrated healing looks like.

There are all sorts of fancy names for the theories I have talked about throughout the book which are supported through studies like the ACES Study, but I didn't not want the book to turn into a textbook about theories; I wanted it to be applicable for everyone so that it will be used in classroom and lectures.

Applying What You've Learned

Even though I've shared a lot of specific examples from my life and experiences, the takeaways are applicable to many different types of situations. If a child starts acting out and engaging in risky behaviors and/or has change in behavior, whether you are a teacher, a friend's mom, or whatever the case may be, you can use the information provided in this book to start the process of finding safety and support for the child in need.

We have to choose whether or not we are going to turn our backs on these kids or show love and compassion. We don't have to be a social worker or teacher to let them know that they are special and that someone cares about them.

Remember, this is not a self-help book. If after reading this book it in anyway inspires or encourages you to want to change any of your behavior or the way you see things, it will not be lasting change if you don't address the root issue of whatever the behavior is that concerns you. I tried parenting books, read inspirational quotes, meditated, and focused on spirituality, but what I found helps me and I hope helps others is looking at the roots of social issues.

By understanding how trauma affects different parts of a person, a society, and its systems, we can stop focusing on the symptoms and start focusing on the cause. The best way we can do this is by understanding our own stories and experiences first. That way, when we work to create change, we are doing it from a healthy, solid place. The change we can accomplish in the world is not about us. It is about helping other people to have the same rights, access to services, and opportunities to feel loved. It is about loving them through their own growth or non-growth. It is about showing them that no matter what they deserve to, can be, and will be loved.

Resources and Recommendations

www.sextraffickingprevention.org
This is my website and contact.

everydayfeminism.com/2014/02/10-ways-to-talk-to-your-
kids-about-sexual-abuse
This is a great article on talking to your kids about sexual abuse.

www.gems-girls.org
Girls Education and Mentoring Services. Contains a wealth of
knowledge and exemplifies survivor leadership.

www.polarisproject.com
It has great information and studies around trafficking.

www.mendingthesoul.org
This is the curriculum that I used to overcome my trauma.

www.hollyaustinsmith.com
You can find *Walking Prey* here, which is an in depth look at
trafficking in the US.

www.acestoohigh.com
This site provides information on the effects of trauma.

www.trustaz.org
Filed with trafficking resources, including downloadable PDF's
for mental health professionals, EMT's, medical professional,
and parents.

www.wingedhope.org
Winged Hope has important information on child abuse prevention.

www.nationalsurvivornetwork.org
This is a great resource for survivors to get connected with other survivors.

www.rebeccabenderministires.org
This is an online mentoring program created by survivors for survivors.

www.safeactionproject.org
This is a hotel and lodging training program to recognize and report human trafficking.

www.brainconnection.com
Provides information about how the brain works and how people learn.

www.childtrauma.org
Collaborative of individuals and organizations working to improve the lives of high-risk children through direct service, research and education.

www.nctsnet.og
The National Child Traumatic Stress Network was established to improve access to care, treatment, and services for traumatized children and adolescents exposed to traumatic events.

www.CcTCkids.org

The Children's Crisis Treatment Center provide a full array of high-quality, comprehensive mental health services to children and their families in Philadelphia, including trauma-focused therapy to children 18 months through 13 years.

www.zerotothree.org

This site offers a comprehensive interactive resource for parents and early childhood education professional on healthy development of children ages zero to three.

www.healthyparent.org

This site offers child development information and divorce-specific information for parents and professionals.

www.trauma-pages.com/bookstore.php

This award-winning site is to provide information for clinicians and researchers in the traumatic-stress field.

Endnotes

Introduction

1 US Department of State, "Definitions," *State.gov,* http://2001-2009.state.gov/g/tip/c16507.htm (accessed 16 July 2015).

2 United Nations Office on Drugs and Crime, "Transnational organized crime: the globalized illegal economy," *UNODC,* http://www.unodc.org/toc/en/crimes/organized-crime.html (accessed 16 July 2015).

3 Nita Bhalla and Reuters, "'Modern-day slavery': State Dept. says millions of human trafficking victims go unidentified," *NBC News,* http://usnews.nbcnews.com (accessed 16 July 2015).

4 National Center for Prosecution of Child Abuse, "CASE Campaign Against Sexual Exploitation," *National District Attorneys Association,* http://www.ndaa.org/ncpca_case_campaign.html (accessed 16 July 2015).

5 National Runaway Safeline, "Frequently Asked Questions," NRS, http://www.1800runaway.org/about-us/faq/ (accessed 16 July 2015).

Chapter 1

1 Shared Hope, "What is Sex Trafficking?," Shared Hope International, http://sharedhope.org/learn/what-is-sex-trafficking/ (accessed 16 July 2015).

2 http://www.sexhelp.com/am-i-a-sex-addict/trauma-bonding

3 Shared Hope, "What is Sex Trafficking?," Shared Hope International, http://sharedhope.org/learn/what-is-sex-trafficking/ (accessed 16 July 2015).

Chapter 2

1

2 Centers for Disease Control. (n.d.). About the Study|Child Maltreatment|Violence Prevention|Injury Center|CDC. Retrieved from http://www.cdc.gov/violenceprevention/acestudy/about.html

3 www.http://acestoohigh.com/aces-101/

4 http://www.acestoohigh.com

5 Stop It Now, "Defining Child Sexual Abuse," *Stop It Now!*, http://www.stopitnow.org/ohc-content/defining-child-sexual-abuse (accessed 16 July 2015).

6 Family Violence Shelter, "Types of Abuse," *Change is Possible (CHIPS)*, http://www.chipsfvs.org/did-you-know.html (accessed 16 July 2015).

7 http://www.thehotline.org/2014/05/what-is-gaslighting/

8 http://www.acf.hhs.gov/programs/cb/research-data-technology/reporting-systems/ncands

9 American Humane Association, "Child Neglect," AHA, http://www.americanhumane.org/ (accessed 16 July 2015).

10 Sasha Cordner, "AG Bondi, Human Trafficking Council Identify Areas That Still Need Work," WFSU, http://news.wfsu.org/post/ag-bondi-human-trafficking-council-identify-areas-still-need-work (accessed 16 July 2015).

Chapter 3

1 Do Something, "11 Facts About Child Abuse," *DoSomething. org*, https://www.dosomething.org/facts/11-facts-about-child-abuse (accessed 16 July 2015).

Acknowledgments

Thank you, Megan Hunter, for taking a chance on this book and supporting me through this incredible journey. I couldn't imagine publishing a book with anyone else. Thank you, Victoria Simons and Jeremy Shapiro, for working seamlessly with and putting up with my million and one commas. Thank you, Gordan Blazevik, for designing the perfect, non-sensationalized cover. Thank you, Cathy Broberg, for helping me organize my words and thoughts in a way that makes sense to the rest of the world.

Thank you to my family for putting up with me through this process and supporting all of my adventures.

Thank you to my husband who has loved me and supported on my worst days and my best, who may never read this book because he has had the audio version on repeat for the last 12 years, and loves me regardless. Thank you, Shaolin, my beautiful daughter, for allowing me to be your mom. You make me proud every day and I love you even though you are funnier than me. For my brilliant Sierra, my little feminist, thank you for showing me what it looks like to love yourself for being exactly who you are and never caring what other people say you should be. To my Sagie, you brighten this world with your love and compassion, and you are proud of everyone around you even when they mess up. You have taught me more about love than I could ever express in words or in this book. Thank you for always being proud of your mommy, and yes, you can be the first to buy it. Drake, thank you for making me laugh and for making my heart melt every day.

To my many mentors and friends who have supported me with grace and unconditional love even when only knowing me for a short time, most of my growth has come from spending time in community with you: Celestia Tracy, Shanell Bender, Blanca Bertrand, Katie Resendiz, Sarah Parks, Kimberly Klein, Phyllis Hill, Dagny Mallory, and Jessica Nicely.

To my best friends who have laughed and cried with me: Amy Johnson, Joanna Robinson, Audrey Sanders, Sarah Parker, Leticia Velasquez and my Angie.

To my many parents. To my one and only Daddy; you are my everything. Thank you for being my biggest cheerleader forever and always. To my moms who have all influenced me and shown me what it is to be a strong woman no matter what life throws at you. To all of the safe adults I had growing up. You are the reason I am here and able to write this book. Thank you.

About the Author

Savannah J. Sanders is a leading advocate in the prevention of child sex trafficking. A survivor of hardships, abuse, and trafficking, Savannah is now living a full life as a victim's advocate, wife, and mother of four. She is currently pursuing a master's degree in social work and is working with the Sandra Day O'Connor Institute as Training Coordinator for the SAFE (Safeguarding Adolescents From Exploitation) Action Project. Sanders shares her story and speaks regularly to groups across the United States on anti-trafficking efforts and ways to support victims.

Her website is: www.sextraffickingprevention.org.